THE MAN WHO WROTE HIS AUTOBIOGRAPHY BEFORE HE WAS BORN

출생 전에 자서전을 쓴 사람

| 조명수 (Ronald M.S. Cho, Ph. D.) 지음 |

쿰란출판사

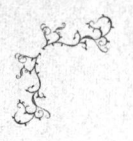

서 문

지난 수천 년의 세월 동안 이 지구에 수많은 사람들이 태어났다. 그렇지만 지금부터 약 2천 년 전 이 세상에 태어나 33년 반 동안 살았던 특별한 사람이 있었다. 그는 태어나기 오래 전부터 자기의 일생을 여러 사람에게 영감을 주어 기록해 놓았다. 예언한 대로 그는 이 세상에 태어났고 그가 기록한 자신의 삶에 대하여 예언된 사건들은 모두 다 그의 생애에서 성취되었다.

출생 전에 자서전을 쓴 특별한 사람의 이름은 예수이며 그의 자서전은 구약과 신약으로 구성된 성경에서 발견된다. 그는 구약에서 예언한 대로 유대 땅 베들레헴에서 출생했으며 이 땅에서 살다가 승천하였다. 그는 신약 성경의 저자들을 통해서 그의 생애에 대하여 기록한 예언들이 어떻게 성취되었는지에 관한 내용뿐만 아니라 장차 이루어질 일들을 기록하였다.

현재까지의 예언들은 모두 성취되었으므로 아직 이루어지지 않은 예언들도 장차 꼭 성취될 것은 분명한 사실이다. 우리는 불확실한 세계에서 살고 있지만 출생 전에 자서전을 쓴 사람을 바로 알고 믿음으로써 이 지구의 과거와 현재와 미래를 알게 되며 삶의 확신과 보증을 갖게 된다. 그러므로 나는 모든 사람이 출생 전에 자서전

PREFACE

Billions of people have been born into this world throughout thousands of years. However, there was an extraordinary man who was born about two thousand years ago and lived for nearly thirty three and a half years. Throughout the many years before he was born, he inspired various people to write about his life. As prophesied, he was born into the world, and all the predicted events of his life which were written about him were fulfilled.

The name of the man who wrote his autobiography before he was born is Jesus, and his autobiography is found in the Bible, composed of the Old and New Testaments. As prophesied in the Old Testament, he was born in Bethlehem, in the land of Judah, and ascended to heaven after his time on earth. Through the authors of the New Testament, he not only wrote how the prophecies of his life were fulfilled but also about future events.

Since all the prophecies leading up to the present have been fulfilled, it is evident that the prophecies regarding events still future will also come to fulfillment. We live in a world of uncer-

을 쓴 사람에 관하여 잘 알 수 있도록 이 재료를 준비하였다. 부디 이 소책자의 독자들은 수많은 성경의 예언들과 성취들을 주의 깊게 연구함으로써 출생 전에 자서전을 쓴 이 사람을 통하여 궁극적이고 영원한 행복을 소유하기를 바라는 바다.

2017년 9월

조명수

tainty, yet through knowing and believing in Jesus, we can gain certainty and assurance for life as we learn of our earth's past, present, and future condition. Therefore, I prepared this resource so that everyone might know about the man who wrote his autobiography before he was born. It is my prayer that through careful study of the Bible's numerous prophecies and their fulfillment the readers of this booklet will receive the ultimate and eternal happiness from the man who wrote his autobiography before he was born.

September 2017
Ronald M.S. Cho

차 례(contents)

- 서문 … 2
  Preface … 3

Chapter 1 — 그의 족보 / His Genealogy …… 8 / 9

Chapter 2 — 그의 출생 / His Birth …… 18 / 19

Chapter 3 — 그의 사역 / His Ministry …… 26 / 27

Chapter 4 — 불신, 거절당함 / Distrust and Rejection …… 54 / 55

Chapter 5 — 범죄자로 고소당함 / Accused of being a Criminal …… 70 / 71

Chapter 6 — 범죄자로서 십자가에 달림 / Crucified as a Criminal …… 74 / 75

Chapter 7 — 십자가에서 운명함 / Death at the Cross …… 90 / 91

Chapter 8 — 부활, 승천하심 / Resurrection & Ascension …… 102 / 103

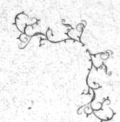

| Chapter 9 | 승천 후 하늘에서 봉사함
Ministry in Heaven after the Ascension | 108
109 |

| Chapter 10 | 재림 전 마지막 7재앙에서 의인들을 보호하심
Protecting the Righteous Ones from the Seven Last Plagues before the Second Coming | 120

121 |

| Chapter 11 | 세상에 다시 강림함(재림)
Returning to Earth: The Second Coming | 138
139 |

| Chapter 12 | 재림 후 하늘에서 1000년간 성도들과 함께 심판하며 왕으로 계심
Being a King and Judging with the Saints for 1000 Years in Heaven after the Second Coming | 158

159 |

| Chapter 13 | 천년 후 지구로 돌아옴(세 번째 강림)
Return to the Earth after the 1000 Years: the Third Coming | 162
163 |

| Chapter 14 | 새 하늘과 새 땅을 창조하심
Creation of New Heaven and Earth | 172
173 |

■ 최고의 기쁜 소식(The Best Good News) … 178

■ 호소(Appeal) … 182

장 1 그의 족보

사 건	예언	역사적 연대	성취	역사적 연대
1. 여자의 후손 : 첫 복음과 성육신의 목적	*창세기 3:15	c. 4000 B.C.	갈라디아서 4:4-5 히브리서 2:14-15 요한일서 3:8-9	c. 4 B.C.
2. 아브라함의 후손	창세기 22:8	c. 1800 B.C.	갈라디아서 3:16	c. 4 B.C.
3. 야곱의 후손	민수기 24:17	c. 1410 B.C.	마태복음 1:2, 16	c. 4 B.C.
4. 유다 지파에서 출생	창세기 49:10	c. 1689 B.C.	누가복음 3:23-33	c. 4 B.C.
5. 다윗의 왕권을 영원히 상속함	*이사야 9:6-7	c. 734 B.C.	누가복음 1:31-33	c. A.D. 27

1. 여자의 후손 : 첫 복음과 성육신의 목적

예언 c. 4000 B.C.

창세기 3:15 — 『내가 너로 여자와 원수가 되게 하고 너의 후손도 여자의 후손과 원수가 되게 하리니 여자의 후손은 네 머리를 상하게 할 것이요 너는 그의 발꿈치를 상하게 할 것

---

*창세기 3:15 – 예수는 인류의 대표자로서 죄와 기만의 창시자인 사단 (요한계시록 12:9)과 싸울 것으로 예언되었다. "그는 너의 머리를 상하게 할 것이요", 이 내용은 불못 (마태복음 25:41 & 요한계시록 20:10)에서 사단이 멸망될 것을 가리키는 것이다. "너는 그의 발꿈치를 상하게 할 것이요", 이 내용은 십자가에서의 예수의 죽음과 3일 후의 부활을 가리키는 것이다.

Chapter 1

His Genealogy

Event	Prophecy	Chronology	Fulfillment	Chronology
1. Her Seed: The First Gospel and Purpose of the Incarnation	*Genesis 3:15	c. 4000 B.C.	Galatians 4:4-5 Hebrews 2:14-15 1John 3:8-9	c. 4 B.C.
2. Abraham's Seed	Genesis 22:8	c. 1800 B.C.	Galatians 3:16	c. 4 B.C.
3. Jacob's Seed	Numbers 24:17	c. 1410 B.C.	Matthew 1:2, 16	c. 4 B.C.
4. Born from the tribe of Judah	Genesis 49:10	c. 1689 B.C.	Luke 3:23-33	c. 4 B.C.
5. Inheritance of David's Throne Forever	*Isaiah 9:6-7	c. 734 B.C.	Luke 1:31-33	c. A.D. 27

 ## 1. Her Seed: The First Gospel and Purpose of the Incarnation

PROPHECY   c. 4000 B.C.

*Genesis 3:15 — And I will put enmity between you and the woman, and between your offspring and hers; he will crush your head, and you will strike his heel.

---

*Genesis 3:15 — Jesus as the representative of humankind was prophesied to fight with Satan, the originator of sin and deception (Revelation 12:9). "…he [Jesus] will crush your head" refers to the defeat of Satan at the cross (John 12:31-33) and ultimately his destruction in the lake of fire Matthew 25:41; Revelation 20:10). "…you [Satan] will strike his heel" refers to Jesus' death on the cross and His resurrection after hree days.

이니라 하시고』

> 성취

c. 4 B.C.

> 갈라디아서 4:4-5 -『때가 차매 하나님이 그 아들을 보내사 여자에게서 나게 하시고 율법 아래 나게 하신 것은 율법 아래에 있는 자들을 속량하시고 우리로 아들의 명분을 얻게 하려 하심이라』

> 히브리서 2:14-15 -『자녀들은 혈육에 함께 속하였으매 그도 또한 한 모양으로 혈육에 함께 속하심은 사망으로 말미암아 사망의 세력을 잡은 자 곧 마귀를 없이 하시며 또 죽기를 무서워하므로 일생에 매여 종 노릇 하는 모든 자들을 놓아주려 하심이니』

> 요한일서 3:8-9 -『죄를 짓는 자는 마귀에게 속하나니 마귀는 처음부터 범죄함이니라 하나님의 아들이 나타나신 것은 마귀의 일을 멸하려 하심이니라 하나님께로부터 난 자마다 죄를 짓지 아니하나니 이는 하나님의 씨가 그의 속에 거함이요 그도 범죄치 못하는 것은 하나님께로서 났음이라』

FULFILLMENT　c. 4 B.C.

Galatians 4:4-5 — But when the time had fully come, God sent his Son, born of a woman, born under law, to redeem those under law, that we might receive the full rights of sons.

Hebrews 2:14-15 — Since the children have flesh and blood, he too shared in their humanity so that by his death he might destroy him who holds the power of death--that is, the devil and free those who all their lives were held in slavery by their fear of death.

1John 3:8-9 — He who does what is sinful is of the devil, because the devil has been sinning from the beginning. The reason the Son of God appeared was to destroy the devil's work. No one who is born of God will continue to sin, because God's seed remains in him; he cannot go on sinning, because he has been born of God.

2. 아브라함의 후손

예언 c. 1800 B.C.

창세기 22:8 －『아브라함이 가로되 아들아 번제할 어린 양은 하나님이 자기를 위하여 친히 준비하시리라 하고 두 사람이 함께 나아가서』

성취 c. 4 B.C.

갈라디아서 3:16 －『이 약속들은 아브라함과 그 자손에게 말씀하신 것인데 여럿을 가리켜 그 자손들이라 하지 아니하시고 오직 하나를 가리켜 네 자손이라 하셨으니 곧 그리스도라』

3. 야곱의 후손

예언 c. 1410 B.C.

민수기 24:17 －『내가 그를 보아도 이 때의 일이 아니며 내가 그를 바라보아도 가까운 일이 아니로다 한 별이 야곱에게서 나오며 한 홀이 이스라엘에게서 일어나서 모압을 이편에서 저편까지 쳐서 파하고 또 소동하는 자식들을 다 멸하리로다』

2. Abraham's Seed

PROPHECY c. 1800 B.C.

> Genesis 22:8 — Abraham answered, "God himself will provide the lamb for the burnt offering, my son." And the two of them went on together.

FULFILLMENT c. 4 B.C.

> Galatians 3:16 — The promises were spoken to Abraham and to his seed. The Scripture does not say "and to seeds," meaning many people, but "and to your seed," meaning one person, who is Christ.

 3. Jacob's Seed

PROPHECY c. 1410 B.C.

> Numbers 24:17 — I see him, but not now; I behold him, but not near. A star will come out of Jacob; a scepter will rise out of Israel. He will crush the foreheads of Moab, the skulls of all the sons of Sheth.

`성 취` c. 4 B.C.

`마태복음 1:2, 16` －『[2] 아브라함이 이삭을 낳고 이삭은 야곱을 낳고 야곱은 유다와 그의 형제를 낳고 … [16] 야곱은 마리아의 남편 요셉을 낳았으니 마리아에게서 그리스도라 칭하는 예수가 나시니라』

🌳 4. 유다지파에서 출생

`예 언` c. 1689 B.C.

`창세기 49:10` －『홀이 유다를 떠나지 아니하며 치리자의 지팡이가 그 발 사이에서 떠나지 아니하시기를 실로가 오시기까지 미치리니 그에게 모든 백성이 복종하리로다』

`성 취` c. 4 B.C.

`누가복음 3:23-33` －『[23] 예수께서 가르치심을 시작할 때에 삼십 세쯤 되시니라 사람들의 아는 대로는 요셉의 아들이니 요셉의 이상은 헬리요 … [33] 그 이상은 아미나답이요 … 그 이상은 유다요』

FULFILLMENT   c. 4 B.C.

Matthew 1:2, 16 — [2] Abraham was the father of Isaac, Isaac the father of Jacob, Jacob the father of Judah and his brothers, [16] and Jacob the father of Joseph, the husband of Mary, of whom was born Jesus, who is called Christ.

4. Born from the tribe of Judah

PROPHECY   c. 1689 B.C.

Genesis 49:10 — The scepter will not depart from Judah, nor the ruler's staff from between his feet, until he comes to whom it belongs and the obedience of the nations is his.

FULFILLMENT   c. 4 B.C.

Luke 3:23–33 — [23] Now Jesus himself was about thirty years old when he began his ministry. He was the son, so it was thought, of Joseph, the son of Heli, ⋯ [33] the son of Amminadab, ⋯ the son of Judah.

5. 다윗의 왕권을 영원히 상속함

예언　c. 734 B.C.

*이사야 9:6-7 — 『이는 한 아기가 우리에게 났고 한 아들을 우리에게 주신 바 되었는데 그의 어깨에는 정사를 메었고 그의 이름은 기묘자라, 모사라, 전능하신 하나님이라, 영존하시는 아버지라, 평강의 왕이라 할 것임이라 그 정사와 평강의 더함이 무궁하며 또 다윗의 위에 앉아서 그 나라를 굳게 세우고 지금 이후 영원토록 공평과 정의로 그것을 보존하실 것이라 만군의 여호와의 열심이 이를 이루시리라』

성취　c. A.D. 27

누가복음 1:31-33 — 『보라 네가 수태하여 아들을 낳으리니 그 이름을 예수라 하라 저가 큰 자가 되고 지극히 높으신 이의 아들이라 일컬을 것이요 주 하나님께서 그 조상 다윗의 위를 저에게 주시리니 영원히 야곱의 집에 왕노릇하실 것이며 그 나라가 무궁하리라』

---

*이사야 9:6-7 — 예수는 다윗의 후손 (로마서 1:3)으로 태어날 것이며 그의 부활과 승천 그리고 하늘에서 보좌에 앉은 후 영원한 왕국을 유업으로 얻을 것이라고 예언되었다.
*별도 표시되지 않으면, 영어 성경 인용은 New King James Version이다. 판권 Copyright ⓒ 1982 by Thomas Nelson, Inc. 사용 허락 받음. 판권 소유.

5. Inheritance of David's Throne Forever

PROPHECY c. 734 B.C.

*Isaiah 9:6–7 — For to us a child is born, to us a son is given, and the government will be on his shoulders. And he will be called Wonderful Counselor, Mighty God, Everlasting Father, Prince of Peace. Of the increase of his government and peace there will be no end. He will reign on David's throne and over his kingdom, establishing and upholding it with justice and righteousness from that time on and forever. The zeal of the LORD Almighty will accomplish this.

FULFILLMENT c. A.D. 27

Luke 1:31–33 — You will be with child and give birth to a son, and you are to give him the name Jesus. He will be great and will be called the Son of the Most High. The Lord God will give him the throne of his father David, and he will reign over the house of Jacob forever; his kingdom will never end."

---

*Isaiah 9:7 — Jesus was prophesied to be born as a descendent of David (Romans 1:3) and inherit the eternal kingdom after His resurrection, ascension, and enthronement in heaven.
*All scripture quotations, unless otherwise indicated, are taken from the New King James Version. Copyright © 1982 by Thomas Nelson, Inc. Used by permission, All rights reserved.

장 2 그의 출생

사 건	예언	역사적 연대	성취	역사적 연대
1. 처녀에게서 태어나며 임마누엘이라 부를것임	*이사야 7:14	c. 734 B.C.	*마태복음 1:21-23	c. 4 B.C.
2. 예정된 장소(베들레헴)에서 출생	미가 5:2	c. 700 B.C.	마태복음 2:5-6	c. 4 B.C.
3. 애굽으로 도피함	호세아 11:1	c. 760 B.C.	마태복음 2:15	c. 4 B.C.
4 어린이들이 학살당함	예레미야 31:15	c. 596 B.C.	마태복음 2:16-18	c. 4 B.C.

1. 처녀에게서 태어나며 임마누엘이라 부를것임

예언 c. 734 B.C.

*이사야 7:14 - 『그러므로 주께서 친히 징조로 너희에게 주실 것이라 보라 처녀가 잉태하여 아들을 낳을 것이요 그 이름을 임마누엘이라 하리라』

---

*이사야 7:14 - 하나님께서는 예수가 신비스러운 출생을 통하여 "여인의 후손"(창세기 3:15)으로 탄생할 것을 징조로 주셨다.
*마태복음 1:21-23 - "하나님이 우리와 함께 계시다"라는 뜻의 임마누엘은 처녀에게서 태어난 예수가 성육신한 하나님임을 나타낸다. (참고 이사야 9:6-7)

Chapter 2 His Birth

Event	Prophecy	Chronology	Fulfillment	Chronology
1. Virgin Birth, Shall be called Immanuel	*Isaiah 7:14	c. 734 B.C.	*Matthew 1:21-23	c. 4 B.C.
2. Born in Prophesied Location(Bethlehem)	Micah 5:2	c. 700 B.C.	Matthew 2:5-6	c. 4 B.C.
3. Escape to Egypt	Hosea 11:1	c. 760 B.C.	Matthew 2:15	c. 4 B.C.
4. Slaughtered Children	Jeremiah 31:15	c. 596 B.C.	Matthew 2:16-18	c. 4 B.C.

 1. Virgin Birth, Shall be called Immanuel

PROPHECY   c. 734 B.C.

Isaiah 7:14 — Therefore the Lord himself will give you a sign : The virgin will be with child and will give birth to a son, and will call him Immanuel.

---

* Isaiah 7:14 — God gave a sign that Jesus would come from "her seed" (Genesis 3:15) through the miraculous nature of his birth.
* Matt. 1:21-23 — The meaning of Immanuel, "God with us," clearly testifies that Jesus, born of a virgin, was God incarnate (cf. Isaiah. 9:6-7).

| 성취 | c. 4 B.C.

*마태복음 1:21-23 -『아들을 낳으리니 이름을 예수라 하라 이는 그가 자기 백성을 저희 죄에서 구원할 자이심이라 하니라 이 모든 일의 된 것은 주께서 선지자로 하신 말씀을 이루려 하심이니 가라사대 보라 처녀가 잉태하여 아들을 낳을 것이요 그 이름은 임마누엘이라 하리라 하셨으니 이를 번역한즉 하나님이 우리와 함께 계시다 함이라』

2. 예정된 장소(베들레헴)에서 출생

| 예언 | c. 700 B.C.

미가 5:2 -『베들레헴 에브라다야 너는 유다 족속 중에 작을지라도 이스라엘을 다스릴 자가 네게서 내게로 나올 것이라 그의 근본은 상고에, 태초에니라』

| 성취 | c. 4 B.C.

마태복음 2:5-6 -『가로되 유대 베들레헴이오니 이는 선지자로 이렇게 기록된 바 또 유대 땅 베들레헴아 너는 유대 고을 중에 가장 작지 아니하도다 네게서 한 다스리는 자가 나와서 내 백성 이스라엘의 목자가 되리라 하였음이니이다』

FULFILLMENT c. 4 B.C.

*Matthew 1:21–23 — She will give birth to a son, and you are to give him the name Jesus, because he will save his people from their sins." All this took place to fulfill what the Lord had said through the prophet: "The virgin will be with child and will give birth to a son, and they will call him Immanuel"--which means, "God with us."

2. Born in Prophesied Location(Bethlehem)

PROPHECY c. 700 B.C.

Micah 5:2 — "But you, Bethlehem Ephrathah, though you are small among the clans of Judah, out of you will come for me one who will be ruler over Israel, whose origins are from of old, from ancient times."

FULFILLMENT c. 4 B.C.

Matthew 2:5–6 — "In Bethlehem in Judea," they replied, "for this is what the prophet has written : "But you, Bethlehem, in the land of Judah, are by no means least among the rulers of Judah ; for out of you will come a ruler who will be the shepherd of my people Israel."

🌱 3. 애굽으로 도피함

예언 c. 760 B.C.

　호세아 11:1 — 『이스라엘의 어렸을 때에 내가 사랑하여 내 아들을 애굽에서 불러내었거늘』

성취 c. 4 B.C.

　마태복음 2:15 — 『헤롯이 죽기까지 거기 있었으니 이는 주께서 선지자로 말씀하신 바 애굽에서 내 아들을 불렀다 함을 이루려 하심이니라』

🌱 4. 어린이들이 학살당함

예언 c. 596 B.C.

　예레미야 31:15 — 『나 여호와가 이같이 말하노라 라마에서 슬퍼하며 통곡하는 소리가 들리니 라헬이 그 자식을 위하여 애곡하는 것이라 그가 자식이 없으므로 위로받기를 거절하는도다』

성취 c. 4 B.C.

　마태복음 2:16-18 — 『이에 헤롯이 박사들에게 속은 줄을 알고 심히 노하여 사람을 보내어 베들레헴과 그 모든 지경 안에 있는 사내아이를 박사들에게 자세히 알아본 그 때를 표준하여 두 살부터 그 아래로 다 죽이니 이에 선지자 예레미야로 말씀

3. Escape to Egypt

PROPHECY c. 760 B.C.

Hosea 11:1 — "When Israel was a child, I loved him, and out of Egypt I called my son.

FULFILLMENT c. 4 B.C.

Matthew 2:15 — where he stayed until the death of Herod. And so was fulfilled what the Lord had said through the prophet : "Out of Egypt I called my son."

 4. Slaughtered Children

PROPHECY c. 596 B.C.

Jeremiah 31:15 — This is what the LORD says : "A voice is heard in Ramah, mourning and great weeping, Rachel weeping for her children and refusing to be comforted, because her children are no more."

FULFILLMENT c. 4 B.C.

Matthew 2:16–18 — When Herod realized that he had been outwitted by the Magi, he was furious, and he gave orders to kill all the boys in Bethlehem and its vicinity who were two years old and under, in accordance with the time he

하신 바 라마에서 슬퍼하며 크게 통곡하는 소리가 들리니 라헬이 그 자식을 위하여 애곡하는 것이라 그가 자식이 없으므로 위로 받기를 거절하였도다 함이 이루어졌느니라』

had learned from the Magi. Then what was said through the prophet Jeremiah was fulfilled : "A voice is heard in Ramah, weeping and great mourning, Rachel weeping for her children and refusing to be comforted, because they are no more."

장 3 그의 사역

사 건	예언	역사적 연대	성취	역사적 연대
1. 선지자가 예수의 사역을 예비함	이사야 40:3-5	c. 690 B.C.	누가복음 3:3-6	c. A.D. 27
2. 성령으로 기름부음 받음	이사야 61:1	c. 690 B.C.	*누가복음 3:21-22 사도행전 10:38	c. A.D. 27
3. 하나님의 기뻐하는 자	이사야 42:1	c. 734 B.C.	누가복음 3:22	c. A.D. 27
4. 모세와 같은 선지자	신명기 18:15, 18	c. 1410 B.C.	사도행전 3:20-22	c. A.D. 31
5. 메시야(그리스도): 다윗의 자손	시편 110:1	c. 970 B.C.	마태복음 22:43-45	c. A.D. 31
6. 사명 선언문을 이해함	이사야 61:1-2	c. 690 B.C.	누가복음 4:16-21	c. A.D. 30
7. 갈릴리 사역	이사야 9:1-2	c. 734 B.C.	마태복음 4:13, 16	c. A.D. 30
8. 비유로 말함	시편 78:2	c. 970 B.C.	마태복음 13:34-35	c. A.D. 29
9. 겸손히 사역함	이사야 42:2	c. 690 B.C.	마태복음 12:17-19	c. A.D. 30
10. 주의 집을 향한 열심이 충만	시편 69:9	c. 970 B.C.	요한복음 2:17	c. A.D. 29
11. 정의를 사랑함	시편 45:6-7	c. 970 B.C.	히브리서 1:8-9	c. A.D. 30
12. 이적을 행함	이사야 35:6	c. 690 B.C.	마태복음 11:4-6	c. A.D. 29
13. 치료봉사	이사야 53:4	c. 690 B.C.	마태복음 8:17	c. A.D. 29
14. 유아들의 경배를 받음	시편 8:2	c. 970 B.C.	마태복음 21:15-16	c. A.D. 30
15. 모퉁이 돌	시편 118:22-23	c. 970 B.C.	마태복음 21:42	c. A.D. 31
16. 하나님의 충성된 제자 (학생)	이사야 50:4-5	c. 690 B.C.	마가복음 1:35	c. A.D. 27
17. 예루살렘성 입성함	스가랴 9:9	c. 487 B.C.	마가복음 11:7-10	c. A.D. 31
18. 고난받는 종	이사야 50:6	c. 690 B.C.	마태복음 26:67	c. A.D. 31

Chapter 3 His Ministry

Event	Prophecy	Chronology	Fulfillment	Chronology
1. Prophet Prepared for Jesus' Ministry	Isaiah 40:3-5	c. 690 B.C.	Luke 3:3-6	c. A.D. 27
2. Anointed by the Holy Spirit	Isaiah 61:1	c. 690 B.C.	*Luke 3:21-22 Acts 10:38	c. A.D. 27
3. In Whom God Delights	Isaiah 42:1	c. 734 B.C.	Luke 3:22	c. A.D. 27
4. Prophet Like Moses	Deut. 18:15, 18	c. 1410 B.C.	Acts 3:20-22	c. A.D. 31
5. Messiah(Christ): the Son of David	Psalms 110:1	c. 970 B.C.	Matthew 22:43-45	c. A.D. 31
6. Understanding the Mission Statement	Isaiah 61:1-2	c. 690 B.C.	Luke 4:16-21	c. A.D. 30
7. Galilee Ministry	Isaiah 9:1-2	c. 734 B.C.	Matthew 4:13, 16	c. A.D. 30
8. Speaks in Parables	Psalms 78:2	c. 970 B.C.	Matthew 13:34-35	c. A.D. 29
9. Humble Ministry	Isaiah 42:2	c. 690 B.C.	Mathew 12:17-19	c. A.D. 30
10. Full of Zeal for God's House	Psalms 69:9	c. 970 B.C.	John 2:17	c. A.D. 29
11. Loving Righteousness	Psalms 45:6-7	c. 970 B.C.	Hebrews 1:8-9	c. A.D. 30
12. Performing Miracles	Isaiah 35:5-6	c. 690 B.C.	Matthew 11:4-5	c. A.D. 29
13. Healing Ministry	Isaiah 53:4	c. 690 B.C.	Matthew 8:17	c. A.D. 29
14. Being Praised by Children	Psalms 8:2	c. 970 B.C.	Matthew 21:15-16	c. A.D. 30
15. The Cornerstone	Psalms 118:22-23	c. 970 B.C.	Matthew 21:42	c. A.D. 31
16. God's Faithful Disciple (Student)	Isaiah 50:4-5	c. 690 B.C.	Mark 1:35	c. A.D. 27
17. Triumphant Entry to Jerusalem	Zechariah 9:9	c. 487 B.C.	Mark 11:7-10	c. A.D. 31
18. Suffering Servant	Isaiah 50:6	c. 690 B.C.	Matthew 26:67	c. A.D. 31

1. 선지자가 예수의 사역을 예비함

예언 c. 690 B.C.

이사야 40:3-5 -『외치는 자의 소리여 가로되 너희는 광야에서 여호와의 길을 예비하라 사막에서 우리 하나님의 대로를 평탄케 하라 골짜기마다 돋우어지며 산마다, 작은 산마다 낮아지며 고르지 않은 곳이 평탄케 되며 험한 곳이 평지가 될 것이요 여호와의 영광이 나타나고 모든 육체가 그것을 함께 보리라 대저 여호와의 입이 말씀하셨느니라』

성취 c. A.D. 27

누가복음 3:3-6 -『요한이 요단 강 부근 각처에 와서 죄 사함을 얻게 하는 회개의 세례를 전파하니 선지자 이사야의 책에 쓴 바 광야에 외치는 자의 소리가 있어 가로되 너희는 주의 길을 예비하라 그의 첩경을 평탄케 하라 모든 골짜기가 메워지고 모든 산과 작은 산이 낮아지고 굽은 것이 곧아지고 험한 길이 평탄하여질 것이요 모든 육체가 하나님의 구원하심을 보리라 함과 같으니라』

1. Prophet Prepared for Jesus' Ministry

PROPHECY c. 690 B.C.

Isaiah 40:3-5 — A voice of one calling : "In the desert prepare the way for the LORD; make straight in the wilderness a highway for our God. Every valley shall be raised up, every mountain and hill made low; the rough ground shall become level, the rugged places a plain. And the glory of the LORD will be revealed, and all mankind together will see it. For the mouth of the LORD has spoken."

FULFILLMENT c. A.D. 27

Luke 3:3-6 — He went into all the country around the Jordan, preaching a baptism of repentance for the forgiveness of sins. As is written in the book of the words of Isaiah the prophet : "A voice of one calling in the desert, 'Prepare the way for the Lord, make straight paths for him. Every valley shall be filled in, every mountain and hill made low. The crooked roads shall become straight, the rough ways smooth. And all mankind will see God's salvation.'"

2. 성령으로 기름부음 받음

예언 c. 690 B.C.

이사야 61:1 —『주 여호와의 신이 내게 임하셨으니 이는 여호와께서 내게 기름을 부으사 가난한 자에게 아름다운 소식을 전하게 하려 하심이라 나를 보내사 마음이 상한 자를 고치며 포로 된 자에게 자유를, 갇힌 자에게 놓임을 전파하며』

성취 c. A.D. 27

*누가복음 3:21-22 —『백성이 다 세례를 받을새 예수도 세례를 받으시고 기도하실 때에 하늘이 열리며 성령이 형체로 비둘기 같이 그의 위에 강림하시더니 하늘로서 소리가 나기를 너는 내 사랑하는 아들이라 내가 너를 기뻐하노라 하시니라』

사도행전 10:38 —『하나님이 나사렛 예수에게 성령과 능력을 기름붓듯 하셨으매 저가 두루 다니시며 착한 일을 행하시고 마귀에게 눌린 모든 자를 고치셨으니 이는 하나님이 함께 하셨음이라』

---

*누가복음 3:21-22 – 누가복음에 따르면 예수가 성령을 받은 것은 물에서 나오자마자가 아니라 물에서 나온 후에 그가 이사야 61:1에 예언한 대로 그의 하나님께서 준 사명을 성공적으로 수행할 수 있도록 기도할 때였다.

2. Anointed by the Holy Spirit

PROPHECY c. 690 B.C.

Isaiah 61:1 — The Spirit of the Sovereign LORD is on me, because the LORD has anointed me to preach good news to the poor. He has sent me to bind up the brokenhearted, to proclaim freedom for the captives and release from darkness for the prisoners,

FULFILLMENT c. A.D. 27

*Luke 3:21-22 — When all the people were being baptized, Jesus was baptized too. And as he was praying, heaven was opened and the Holy Spirit descended on him in bodily form like a dove. And a voice came from heaven : "You are my Son, whom I love; with you I am well pleased."

Acts 10:38 — how God anointed Jesus of Nazareth with the Holy Spirit and power, and how he went around doing good and healing all who were under the power of the devil, because God was with him.

---

*Luke 3:21-22 — According to the gospel of Luke, Jesus did not receive the Holy Spirit immediately after coming up from the water, but afterwards while He was praying for the successful fulfillment of His God- given mission as prophesied in Isaiah 61:1-3.

🌳 3. 하나님의 기뻐하는 자

예언 c. 734 B.C.

> **이사야 42:1** -『내가 붙드는 나의 종, 내 마음에 기뻐하는 나의 택한 사람을 보라 내가 나의 신을 그에게 주었은즉 그가 이방에 공의를 베풀리라』

성취 c. A.D. 27

> **누가복음 3:22** -『성령이 형체로 비둘기 같이 그의 위에 강림하시더니 하늘로서 소리가 나기를 너는 내 사랑하는 아들이라 내가 너를 기뻐하노라 하시니라』

🌳 4. 모세와 같은 선지자

예언 c. 1410 B.C.

> **신명기 18:15, 18** -『[15] 네 하나님 여호와께서 너의 중 네 형제 중에서 나와 같은 선지자 하나를 너를 위하여 일으키시리니 너희는 그를 들을지니라 [18] 내가 그들의 형제 중에 너와 같은 선지자 하나를 그들을 위하여 일으키고 내 말을 그 입에 두리니 내가 그에게 명하는 것을 그가 무리에게 다 고하리라』

성취 c. A.D. 31

> **사도행전 3:20-22** -『또 주께서 너희를 위하여 예정하신 그리

3. In Whom God Delights

PROPHECY c. 734 B.C.

> Isaiah 42:1 — "Here is my servant, whom I uphold, my chosen one in whom I delight; I will put my Spirit on him and he will bring justice to the nations.

FULFILLMENT c. A.D. 27

> Luke 3:22 — and the Holy Spirit descended on him in bodily form like a dove. And a voice came from heaven : "You are my Son, whom I love; with you I am well pleased."

 ## 4. Prophet Like Moses

PROPHECY c. 1410 B.C.

> Deut. 18:15, 18 — [15] The LORD your God will raise up for you a prophet like me from among your own brothers. You must listen to him. [18] I will raise up for them a prophet like you from among their brothers; I will put my words in his mouth, and he will tell them everything I command him.

FULFILLMENT c. A.D. 31

> Acts 3:20–22 — and that he may send the Christ, who has

스도 곧 예수를 보내시리니 하나님이 영원 전부터 거룩한 선지자의 입을 의탁하여 말씀하신 바 만유를 회복하실 때까지는 하늘이 마땅히 그를 받아 두리라 모세가 말하되 주 하나님이 너희를 위하여 너희 형제 가운데서 나 같은 선지자 하나를 세울 것이니 너희가 무엇이든지 그 모든 말씀을 들을 것이라』

🌳 5. 메시아(그리스도) : 다윗의 자손

예언 c. 970 B.C.

　시편 110:1 —『여호와께서 내 주에게 말씀하시기를 내가 네 원수로 네 발등상 되게 하기까지 너는 내 우편에 앉으라 하셨도다』

성취 c. A.D. 31

　마태복음 22:41-45 —『바리새인들이 모였을 때에 예수께서 그들에게 물으시되 너희는 그리스도에 대하여 어떻게 생각하느냐 뉘 자손이냐 대답하되 다윗의 자손이니이다 가라사대 그러면 다윗이 성령에 감동하여 어찌 그리스도를 주라 칭하여 말하되 주께서 내 주께 이르시되 내가 네 원수를 네 발 아래 둘 때까지 내 우편에 앉았으라 하셨도다 하였느냐 다윗이 그리스도를 주라 칭하였은즉 어찌 그의 자손이 되겠느냐 하시니』

been appointed for you even Jesus. He must remain in heaven until the time comes for God to restore everything, as he promised long ago through his holy prophets. For Moses said, 'The Lord your God will raise up for you a prophet like me from among your own people; you must listen to everything he tells you.

5. Messiah(Christ) : the Son of David

PROPHECY   c. 970 B.C.

Psalms 110:1 — The LORD says to my Lord : "Sit at my right hand until I make your enemies a footstool for your feet."

FULFILLMENT   c. A.D. 31

Matthew 22:41–45 — While the Pharisees were gathered together, Jesus asked them, "What do you think about the Christ? Whose son is he?" "The son of David," they replied. He said to them, "How is it then that David, speaking by the Spirit, calls him 'Lord'? For he says, "'The Lord said to my Lord : "Sit at my right hand until I put your enemies under your feet."' If then David calls him 'Lord,' how can he be his son?"

6. 사명 선언문을 이해함

예언   c. 690 B.C.

> 이사야 61:1-2 — 『주 여호와의 신이 내게 임하셨으니 이는 여호와께서 내게 기름을 부으사 가난한 자에게 아름다운 소식을 전하게 하려 하심이라 나를 보내사 마음이 상한 자를 고치며 포로 된 자에게 자유를, 갇힌 자에게 놓임을 전파하며 여호와의 은혜의 해와 우리 하나님의 신원의 날을 전파하여 모든 슬픈 자를 위로하되』

성취   c. A.D. 30

> 누가복음 4:16-21 — 『예수께서 그 자라나신 곳 나사렛에 이르사 안식일에 자기 규례대로 회당에 들어가사 성경을 읽으려고 서시매 선지자 이사야의 글을 드리거늘 책을 펴서 이렇게 기록한 데를 찾으시니 곧 주의 성령이 내게 임하셨으니 이는 가난한 자에게 복음을 전하게 하시려고 내게 기름을 부으시고 나를 보내사 포로된 자에게 자유를, 눈먼 자에게 다시 보게 함을 전파하며 눌린 자를 자유케 하고 주의 은혜의 해를 전파하게 하려 하심이라 하였더라 책을 덮어 그 맡은 자에게 주시고 앉으시니 회당에 있는 자들이 다 주목하여 보더라 이에 예수께서 저희에게 말씀하시되 이 글이 오늘날 너희 귀에 응하였느니라 하시니』

6. Understanding the Mission Statement

PROPHECY c. 690 B.C.

Isaiah 61:1-2 — The Spirit of the Sovereign LORD is on me, because the LORD has anointed me to preach good news to the poor. He has sent me to bind up the brokenhearted, to proclaim freedom for the captives and release from darkness for the prisoners, to proclaim the year of the LORD'S favor and the day of vengeance of our God, to comfort all who mourn,

FULFILLMENT c. A.D. 30

Luke 4:16-21 — He went to Nazareth, where he had been brought up, and on the Sabbath day he went into the synagogue, as was his custom. And he stood up to read. The scroll of the prophet Isaiah was handed to him. Unrolling it, he found the place where it is written : "The Spirit of the Lord is on me, because he has anointed me to preach good news to the poor. He has sent me to proclaim freedom for the prisoners and recovery of sight for the blind, to release the oppressed, to proclaim the year of the Lord's favor." Then he rolled up the scroll, gave it back to the attendant and sat down. The eyes of everyone in the synagogue were fastened on him, and he began by saying to them, "Today this scripture is fulfilled in your hearing.

7. 갈릴리 사역

예언 c. 734 B.C.

이사야 9:1-2 -『전에 고통하던 자에게는 흑암이 없으리로다 옛적에는 여호와께서 스불론 땅과 납달리 땅으로 멸시를 당케 하셨더니 후에는 해변길과 요단 저편 이방의 갈릴리를 영화롭게 하셨느니라 흑암에 행하던 백성이 큰 빛을 보고 사망의 그늘진 땅에 거하던 자에게 빛이 비취도다』

성취 c. A.D. 30

마태복음 4:13, 16 -『[13] 나사렛을 떠나 스불론과 납달리 지경 해변에 있는 가버나움에 가서 사시니 [16] 흑암에 앉은 백성이 큰 빛을 보았고 사망의 땅과 그늘에 앉은 자들에게 빛이 비취었도다 하였느니라』

8. 비유로 말함

예언 c. 970 B.C.

시편 78:2 -『내가 입을 열고 비유를 베풀어서 옛 비밀한 말을 발표하리니』

7. Galilee Ministry

PROPHECY c. 734 B.C.

Isaiah 9:1-2 — Nevertheless, there will be no more gloom for those who were in distress. In the past he humbled the land of Zebulun and the land of Naphtali, but in the future he will honor Galilee of the Gentiles, by the way of the sea, along the Jordan-- The people walking in darkness have seen a great light; on those living in the land of the shadow of death a light has dawned.

FULFILLMENT c. A.D. 30

Matthew 4:13, 16 — [13] Leaving Nazareth, he went and lived in Capernaum, which was by the lake in the area of Zebulun and Naphtali-- [16] the people living in darkness have seen a great light; on those living in the land of the shadow of death a light has dawned."

 8. Speaks in Parables

PROPHECY c. 970 B.C.

Psalms 78:2 — I will open my mouth in parables, I will utter hidden things, things from of old--

성취 c. A.D. 29

마태복음 13:34-35 -『예수께서 이 모든 것을 무리에게 비유로 말씀하시고 비유가 아니면 아무것도 말씀하지 아니하셨으니 이는 선지자로 말씀하신 바 내가 입을 열어 비유로 말하고 창세부터 감추인 것들을 드러내리라 함을 이루려 하심이니라』

9. 겸손히 사역함

예언 c. 690 B.C.

이사야 42:2 -『그는 외치지 아니하며 목소리를 높이지 아니하며 그 소리로 거리에 들리게 아니하며』

성취 c. A.D. 30

마태복음 12:17-19 -『이는 선지자 이사야로 말씀하신 바 보라 나의 택한 종 곧 내 마음에 기뻐하는 바 나의 사랑하는 자로다 내가 내 성령을 줄 터이니 그가 심판을 이방에 알게 하리라 그가 다투지도 아니하며 들레지도 아니하리니 아무도 길에서 그 소리를 듣지 못하리라』

FULFILLMENT c. A.D. 29

Matthew 13:34–35 — Jesus spoke all these things to the crowd in parables; he did not say anything to them without using a parable. So was fulfilled what was spoken through the prophet : "I will open my mouth in parables, I will utter things hidden since the creation of the world."

 9. Humble Ministry

PROPHECY c. 690 B.C.

Isaiah 42:2 — He will not shout or cry out, or raise his voice in the streets.

FULFILLMENT c. A.D. 30

Mathew 12:17–19 — This was to fulfill what was spoken through the prophet Isaiah: "Here is my servant whom I have chosen, the one I love, in whom I delight; I will put my Spirit on him, and he will proclaim justice to the nations. He will not quarrel or cry out; no one will hear his voice in the streets.

🌱 10. 주의 집을 향한 열심이 충만

예언 c. 970 B.C.

　시편 69:9 －『주의 집을 위하는 열성이 나를 삼키고 주를 훼방하는 훼방이 내게 미쳤나이다』

성취 c. A.D. 29

　요한복음 2:17 －『제자들이 성경 말씀에 주의 전을 사모하는 열심이 나를 삼키리라 한 것을 기억하더라』

🌱 11. 정의를 사랑함

예언 c. 970 B.C.

　시편 45:6-7 －『하나님이여 주의 보좌가 영영하며 주의 나라의 홀은 공평한 홀이니이다 왕이 정의를 사랑하고 악을 미워하시니 그러므로 하나님 곧 왕의 하나님이 즐거움의 기름으로 왕에게 부어 왕의 동류보다 승하게 하셨나이다』

성취 c. A.D. 30

　히브리서 1:8-9 －『아들에 관하여는 하나님이여 주의 보좌가 영영하며 주의 나라의 홀은 공평한 홀이니이다 네가 의를 사랑하고 불법을 미워하였으니 그러므로 하나님 곧 너의 하나님이 즐거움의 기름을 네게 부어 네 동류들보다 승하게 하셨

10. Full of Zeal for God's House

PROPHECY c. 970 B.C.

Psalms 69:9 — for zeal for your house consumes me, and the insults of those who insult you fall on me.

FULFILLMENT c. A.D. 29

John 2:17 — His disciples remembered that it is written : "Zeal for your house will consume me."

 11. Prophet Like Moses

PROPHECY c. 970 B.C.

Psalms 45:6–7 — Your throne, O God, will last for ever and ever; a scepter of justice will be the scepter of your kingdom. You love righteousness and hate wickedness; therefore God, your God, has set you above your companions by anointing you with the oil of joy.

FULFILLMENT c. A.D. 30

Hebrews 1:8–9 — But about the Son he says, "Your throne, O God, will last for ever and ever, and righteousness will be the scepter of your kingdom. You have loved righteousness and hated wickedness; therefore God, your God, has set you

도다 하였고』

🌳 12. 이적을 행함

예언 c. 690 B.C.

이사야 35:5-6 -『그 때에 소경의 눈이 밝을 것이며 귀머거리의 귀가 열릴 것이며 그 때에 저는 자는 사슴 같이 뛸 것이며 벙어리의 혀는 노래하리니 이는 광야에서 물이 솟겠고 사막에서 시내가 흐를 것임이라』

성취 c. A.D. 29

마태복음 11:4-6 -『예수께서 대답하여 가라사대 너희가 가서 듣고 보는 것을 요한에게 고하되 소경이 보며 앉은뱅이가 걸으며 문둥이가 깨끗함을 받으며 귀머거리가 들으며 죽은 자가 살아나며 가난한 자에게 복음이 전파된다 하라 누구든지 나를 인하여 실족하지 아니하는 자는 복이 있도다 하시니라』

🌳 13. 치료봉사

예언 c. 690 B.C.

이사야 53:4 -『그는 실로 우리의 질고를 지고 우리의 슬픔을 당하였거늘 우리는 생각하기를 그는 징벌을 받아서 하나님에게 맞으며 고난을 당한다 하였노라』

above your companions by anointing you with the oil of joy."

12. Performing Miracles

PROPHECY c. 690 B.C.

> Isaiah 35:5-6 — Then will the eyes of the blind be opened and the ears of the deaf unstopped. Then will the lame leap like a deer, and the mute tongue shout for joy. Water will gush forth in the wilderness and streams in the desert.

FULFILLMENT c. A.D. 29

> Matthew 11:4-6 — Jesus replied, "Go back and report to John what you hear and see : The blind receive sight, the lame walk, those who have leprosyare cured, the deaf hear, the dead are raised, and the good news is preached to the poor. Blessed is the man who does not fall away on account of me."

13. Healing Ministry

PROPHECY c. 690 B.C.

> Isaiah 53:4 — Surely he took up our infirmities and carried our sorrows, yet we considered him stricken by God, smitten by him, and afflicted.

| 성취 | c. A.D. 29

> 마태복음 8:17 －『이는 선지자 이사야로 하신 말씀에 우리 연약한 것을 친히 담당하시고 병을 짊어지셨도다 함을 이루려 하심이더라』

14. 유아들의 경배를 받음

| 예언 | c. 970 B.C.

> 시편 8:2 －『주의 대적을 인하여 어린 아이와 젖먹이의 입으로 말미암아 권능을 세우심이여 이는 원수와 보수자로 잠잠케 하려 하심이니이다』

| 성취 | c. A.D. 30

> 마태복음 21:15-16 －『대제사장들과 서기관들이 예수의 하시는 이상한 일과 또 성전에서 소리질러 호산나 다윗의 자손이여 하는 아이들을 보고 분하여 예수께 말하되 저희의 하는 말을 듣느뇨 예수께서 가라사대 그렇다 어린 아기와 젖먹이들의 입에서 나오는 찬미를 온전케 하셨나이다 함을 너희가 읽어 본 일이 없느냐 하시고』

`FULFILLMENT` c. A.D. 29

`Matthew 8:17` — This was to fulfill what was spoken through the prophet Isaiah : "He took up our infirmities and carried our diseases."

14. Being Praised by Children

`PROPHECY` c. 970 B.C.

`Psalms 8:2` — From the lips of children and infants you have ordained praise because of your enemies, to silence the foe and the avenger.

`FULFILLMENT` c. A.D. 30

`Matthew 21:15–16` — But when the chief priests and the teachers of the law saw the wonderful things he did and the children shouting in the temple area, "Hosanna to the Son of David," they were indignant. "Do you hear what these children are saying?" they asked him. "Yes," replied Jesus, "have you never read, "'From the lips of children and infants you have ordained praise'?"

15. 모퉁이 돌

예언 c. 970 B.C.

> 시편 118:22-23 - 『건축자의 버린 돌이 집 모퉁이의 머릿돌이 되었나니 이는 여호와의 행하신 것이요 우리 눈에 기이한 바로다』

성취 c. A.D. 31

> 마태복음 21:42 - 『예수께서 가라사대 너희가 성경에 건축자들의 버린 돌이 모퉁이의 머릿돌이 되었나니 이것은 주로 말미암아 된 것이요 우리 눈에 기이하도다 함을 읽어 본 일이 없느냐』

16. 하나님의 충성된 제자(학생)

예언 c. 690 B.C.

> *이사야 50:4-5 - 『주 여호와께서 학자의 혀를 내게 주사 나로 곤핍한 자를 말로 어떻게 도와줄 줄을 알게 하시고 아침마다 깨우치시되 나의 귀를 깨우치사 학자 같이 알아듣게 하시도다』

---

*이사야 50:4-5 - 예수가 그의 사역을 성공적으로 수행할 수 있었던 것은 그가 그의 아버지께 매일 아침마다 하나님의 충실한 제자로서 교육받은 것이었다.

15. The Cornerstone

PROPHECY c. 970 B.C.

Psalms 118:22–23 — The stone the builders rejected has become the capstone; the LORD has done this, and it is marvelous in our eyes.

FULFILLMENT c. A.D. 31

Matthew 21:42 — Jesus said to them, "Have you never read in the Scriptures : "'The stone the builders rejected has become the capstone; the Lord has done this, and it is marvelous in our eyes'?

 16. God's Faithful Disciple(Student)

PROPHECY c. 690 B.C.

*Isaiah 50:4–5 — The Sovereign LORD has given me an instructed tongue, to know the word that sustains the weary. He wakens me morning by morning, wakens my ear to listen like one being taught. The Sovereign LORD has opened my ears, and I have not been rebellious; I have not drawn back.

---

*Isaiah 50:4-5 — Jesus was able to finish His ministry successfully because, as a faithful disciple of God, He was instructed by His Father every morning.

| 성취 | c. A.D. 27

　마가복음 1:35 -『새벽 오히려 미명에 예수께서 일어나 나가 한적한 곳으로 가사 거기서 기도하시더니』

17. 예루살렘성 입성함

| 예언 | c. 487 B.C.

　스가랴 9:9 -『시온의 딸아 크게 기뻐할지어다 예루살렘의 딸아 즐거이 부를지어다 보라 네 왕이 네게 임하나니 그는 공의로우며 구원을 베풀며 겸손하여서 나귀를 타나니 나귀의 작은 것 곧 나귀새끼니라』

| 성취 | c. A.D. 31

　마가복음 11:7-10 -『나귀 새끼를 예수께로 끌고 와서 자기들의 겉옷을 그 위에 걸쳐두매 예수께서 타시니 많은 사람은 자기 겉옷과 다른 이들은 밭에서 벤 나무가지를 길에 펴며 앞에서 가고 뒤에서 따르는 자들이 소리지르되 호산나 찬송하리로다 주의 이름으로 오시는 이여 찬송하리로다 오는 우리 조상 다윗의 나라여 가장 높은 곳에서 호산나 하더라』

FULFILLMENT c. A.D. 27

Mark 1:35 — Very early in the morning, while it was still dark, Jesus got up, left the house and went off to a solitary place, where he prayed.

 17. Triumphant Entry to Jerusalem

PROPHECY c. 487 B.C.

Zechariah 9:9 — Rejoice greatly, O Daughter of Zion! Shout, Daughter of Jerusalem! See, your king comes to you, righteous and having salvation, gentle and riding on a donkey, on a colt, the foal of a donkey.

FULFILLMENT c. A.D. 31

Mark 11:7-10 — When they brought the colt to Jesus and threw their cloaks over it, he sat on it. Many people spread their cloaks on the road, while others spread branches they had cut in the fields. Those who went ahead and those who followed shouted, "Hosanna!" "Blessed is he who comes in the name of the Lord!" "Blessed is the coming kingdom of our father David!" "Hosanna in the highest!"

🌱 18. 고난받는 종

예언 c. 690 B.C.

> **이사야 50:6** －『나를 때리는 자들에게 내 등을 맡기며 나의 수염을 뽑는 자들에게 나의 뺨을 맡기며 수욕과 침 뱉음을 피하려고 내 얼굴을 가리우지 아니하였느니라』

성취 c. A.D. 31

> **마태복음 26:67** －『이에 예수의 얼굴에 침 뱉으며 주먹으로 치고 혹은 손바닥으로 때리며』

18. Suffering Servant

PROPHECY c. 690 B.C.

Isaiah 50:6 — I offered my back to those who beat me, my cheeks to those who pulled out my beard; I did not hide my face from mocking and spitting.

FULFILLMENT c. A.D. 31

Matthew 26:67 — Then they spit in his face and struck him with their fists. Others slapped him

장 4 불신, 거절당함

사 건	예언	역사적 연대	성취	역사적 연대
1. 훼방을 받음	시편 69:7, 9, 20	c. 970 B.C.	로마서 15:3	c. A.D. 31
2. 가족들에게 의심 받음	시편 69:8	c. 970 B.C.	요한복음 7:3-5	c. A.D. 31
3. 오해받음	이사야 6:9-10	c. 940 B.C.	마태복음 3:13-15	c. A.D. 31
4. 무고히 미움 받음	시편 35:19, 69:4	c. 970 B.C.	요한복음 15:24-25	c. A.D. 31
5. 지도자들에게 도전받음	이사야 29:13	c. 730 B.C.	마태복음 15:8-9	c. A.D. 31
6. 유대지도자들에게 거절 당함	시편 118:22	c. 970 B.C.	마가복음 12:10-12	c. A.D. 31
7. 이방인과 유대인에게 대적 당함	시편 2:1-2	c. 970 B.C.	사도행전 4:25-27	c. A.D. 31
8. 제자들에게 버림 받음	스가랴 13:7	c. 487 B.C.	마태복음 26:31, 56	c. A.D. 31
9. 가까운 사람에게 배신당함	시편 41:9	c. 970 B.C.	요한복음 13:18, 21	c. A.D. 31
10. 은 30에 팔림	스가랴 11:12	c. 487 B.C.	마태복음 26:15	c. A.D. 31

1. 훼방을 받음

예언 c. 970 B.C.

> **시편 69:7, 9, 20** — 『[7] 내가 주를 위하여 훼방을 받았사오니 수치가 내 얼굴에 덮였나이다 [9] 주의 집을 위하는 열성이

Chapter 4 Distrust and Rejection

Event	Prophecy	Chronology	Fulfillment	Chronology
1. Being Scorned	Psalms 69:7, 9, 20	c. 970 B.C.	Romans 15:3	c. A.D. 31
2. Doubted by Family	Psalms 69:8	c. 970 B.C.	John 7:3-5	c. A.D. 31
3. Being Misunderstood	Isaiah 6:9-10	c. 940 B.C.	Matthew 13:13-15	c. A.D. 31
4. Hated Without Cause	Psalms 35:19, 69:4	c. 970 B.C.	John 15:24-25	c. A.D. 31
5. Challenged by Leaders	Isaiah 29:13	c. 730 B.C.	Matthew 15:8-9	c. A.D. 31
6. Rejected by Jewish Leaders	Psalms 118:22	c. 970 B.C.	Mark 12:10-12	c. A.D. 31
7. Confronted by Jews and Gentiles	Psalms 2:1-2	c. 970 B.C.	Acts 4:25-27	c. A.D. 31
8. Abandoned by Disciples	Zechariah 13:7	c. 487 B.C.	Matthew 26:31, 56	c. A.D. 31
9. Betrayed by close friend	Psalms 41:9	c. 970 B.C.	John 13:18, 21	c. A.D. 31
10. Sold for 30 Pieces of Silver	Zechariah 11:12	c. 487 B.C.	Matthew 26:15	c. A.D. 31

 1. Being Scorned

PROPHECY c. 970 B.C.

Psalms 69:7, 9, 20 — [7] For I endure scorn for your sake, and shame covers my face. [9] for zeal for your house consumes

나를 삼키고 주를 훼방하는 훼방이 내게 미쳤나이다 [20] 훼방이 내 마음을 상하여 근심이 충만하니 긍휼이 여길 자를 바라나 없고 안위할 자를 바라나 찾지 못하였나이다』

성취 c. A.D. 31

로마서 15:3 -『그리스도께서 자기를 기쁘게 하지 아니하셨나니 기록된 바 주를 비방하는 자들의 비방이 내게 미쳤나이다 함과 같으니라』

2. 가족들에게 의심 받음

예언 c. 970 B.C.

시편 69:8 -『내가 내 형제에게는 객이 되고 내 모친의 자녀에게는 외인이 되었나이다』

성취 c. A.D. 31

요한복음 7:3-5 -『그 형제들이 예수께 이르되 당신의 행하는 일을 제자들도 보게 여기를 떠나 유대로 가소서 스스로 나타나기를 구하면서 묻혀서 일하는 사람이 없나니 이 일을 행하려 하거든 자신을 세상에 나타내소서 하니 이는 그 형제들이라도 예수를 믿지 아니함이러라』

me, and the insults of those who insult you fall on me. [20] Scorn has broken my heart and has left me helpless; I looked for sympathy, but there was none, for comforters, but I found none.

FULFILLMENT c. A.D. 31

Romans 15:3 — For even Christ did not please himself but, as it is written : "The insults of those who insult you have fallen on me."

2. Doubted by Family

PROPHECY c. 970 B.C.

Psalms 69:8 — I am a stranger to my brothers, an alien to my own mother's sons;

FULFILLMENT c. A.D. 31

John 7:3-5 — Jesus' brothers said to him, "You ought to leave here and go to Judea, so that your disciples may see the miracles you do. No one who wants to become a public figure acts in secret. Since you are doing these things, show yourself to the world." For even his own brothers did not believe in him.

3. 오해받음

예언 c. 940 B.C.

> 이사야 6:9-10 ―『여호와께서 가라사대 가서 이 백성에게 이르기를 너희가 듣기는 들어도 깨닫지 못할 것이요 보기는 보아도 알지 못하리라 하여 이 백성의 마음으로 둔하게 하며 그 귀가 막히고 눈이 감기게 하라 염려컨대 그들이 눈으로 보고 귀로 듣고 마음으로 깨닫고 다시 돌아와서 고침을 받을까 하노라』

성취 c. A.D. 31

> 마태복음 13:13-15 ―『그러므로 내가 저희에게 비유로 말하기는 저희가 보아도 보지 못하며 들어도 듣지 못하며 깨닫지 못함이니라 이사야의 예언이 저희에게 이루었으니 일렀으되 너희가 듣기는 들어도 깨닫지 못할 것이요 보기는 보아도 알지 못하리라 이 백성들의 마음이 완악하여져서 그 귀는 듣기에 둔하고 눈은 감았으니 이는 눈으로 보고 귀로 듣고 마음으로 깨달아 돌이켜 내게 고침을 받을까 두려워함이라 하였느니라』

3. Being Misunderstood

PROPHECY   c. 940 B.C.

Isaiah 6:9–10 — He said, "Go and tell this people : "'Be ever hearing, but never understanding; be ever seeing, but never perceiving.' Make the heart of this people calloused; make their ears dull and close their eyes. Otherwise they might see with their eyes, hear with their ears, understand with their hearts, and turn and be healed."

FULFILLMENT   c. A.D. 31

Matthew 13:13–15 — This is why I speak to them in parables : "Though seeing, they do not see; though hearing, they do not hear or understand. In them is fulfilled the prophecy of Isaiah : "'You will be ever hearing but never understanding; you will be ever seeing but never perceiving. For this people's heart has become calloused; they hardly hear with their ears, and they have closed their eyes. Otherwise they might see with their eyes, hear with their ears, understand with their hearts and turn, and I would heal them.'

4. 무고히 미움 받음

예언 c. 970 B.C.

시편 35:19 -『무리하게 나의 원수된 자로 나를 인하여 기뻐하지 못하게 하시며 무고히 나를 미워하는 자로 눈짓하지 못하게 하소서』

시편 69:4 -『무고히 나를 미워하는 자가 내 머리털보다 많고 무리히 내 원수가 되어 나를 끊으려 하는 자가 강하였으니 내가 취치 아니한 것도 물어 주게 되었나이다』

성취 c. A.D. 31

요한복음 15:24-25 -『내가 아무도 못한 일을 저희 중에서 하지 아니하였더면 저희가 죄 없었으려니와 지금은 저희가 나와 및 내 아버지를 보았고 또 미워하였도다 그러나 이는 저희 율법에 기록된 바 저희가 연고 없이 나를 미워하였다 한 말을 응하게 하려 함이니라』

5. 지도자들에게 도전받음

예언 c. 730 B.C.

이사야 29:13 -『주께서 가라사대 이 백성이 입으로는 나를 가까이하며 입술로는 나를 존경하나 그 마음은 내게서 멀리

4. Hated without Cause

PROPHECY   c. 970 B.C.

Psalms 35:19 — Let not those gloat over me who are my enemies without cause; let not those who hate me without reason maliciously wink the eye.

Psalms 69:4 — Those who hate me without reason outnumber the hairs of my head; many are my enemies without cause, those who seek to destroy me. I am forced to restore what I did not steal.

FULFILLMENT   c. A.D. 31

John 15:24–25 — If I had not done among them what no one else did, they would not be guilty of sin. But now they have seen these miracles, and yet they have hated both me and my Father. But this is to fulfill what is written in their Law: 'They hated me without reason.'

 ## 5. Challenged by Leaders

PROPHECY   c. 730 B.C.

Isaiah 29:13 — The Lord says: These people come near to me with their mouth and honor me with their lips, but their

떠났나니 그들이 나를 경외함은 사람의 계명으로 가르침을 받았을 뿐이라』

성취 c. A.D. 31

마태복음 15:8-9 —『이 백성이 입술로는 나를 존경하되 마음은 내게서 멀도다 사람의 계명으로 교훈을 삼아 가르치니 나를 헛되이 경배하는도다 하였느니라 하시고』

6. 유대지도자들에게 거절당함

예언 c. 970 B.C.

시편 118:22 —『건축자의 버린 돌이 집 모퉁이의 머릿돌이 되었나니』

성취 c. A.D. 31

마가복음 12:10-12 —『너희가 성경에 건축자들이 버린 돌이 모퉁이의 머릿돌이 되었나니 이것은 주로 말미암아 된 것이요 우리 눈에 기이하도다 함을 읽어 보지도 못하였느냐 하시니라 저희가 예수의 이 비유는 자기들을 가리켜 말씀하심인 줄 알고 잡고자 하되 무리를 두려워하여 예수를 버려두고 가니라』

hearts are far from me. Their worship of me is made up only of rules taught by men.

FULFILLMENT c. A.D. 31

Matthew 15:8-9 — "These people honor me with their lips, but their hearts are far from me. They worship me in vain; their teachings are but rules taught by men."

6. Rejected by Jewish Leaders

PROPHECY c. 970 B.C.

Psalms 118:22 — The stone the builders rejected has become the capstone;

FULFILLMENT c. A.D. 31

Mark 12:10-12 — Haven't you read this scripture : "'The stone the builders rejected has become the capstone; the Lord has done this, and it is marvelous in our eyes'?" Then they looked for a way to arrest him because they knew he had spoken the parable against them. But they were afraid of the crowd; so they left him and went away.

7. 이방인과 유대인에게 거절당함

예언 c. 970 B.C.

시편 2:1-2 —『어찌하여 열방이 분노하며 민족들이 허사를 경영하는고 세상의 군왕들이 나서며 관원들이 서로 꾀하여 여호와와 그 기름 받은 자를 대적하며』

성취 c. A.D. 31

사도행전 4:25-27 —『또 주의 종 우리 조상 다윗의 입을 의탁하사 성령으로 말씀하시기를 어찌하여 열방이 분노하며 족속들이 허사를 경영하였는고 세상의 군왕들이 나서며 관원들이 함께 모여 주와 그 그리스도를 대적하도다 하신 이로소이다 과연 헤롯과 본디오 빌라도는 이방인과 이스라엘 백성과 합동하여 하나님의 기름부으신 거룩한 종 예수를 거스려』

8. 제자들에게 버림 받음

예언 c. 487 B.C.

스가랴 13:7 —『만군의 여호와가 말하노라 칼아 깨어서 내 목자, 내 짝된 자를 치라 목자를 치면 양이 흩어지려니와 작은 자들 위에는 내가 내 손을 드리우리라』

7. Confronted by Jews and Gentiles

PROPHECY   c. 970 B.C.

Psalms 2:1-2 — Why do the nations conspire and the peoples plot in vain? The kings of the earth take their stand and the rulers gather together against the LORD and against his Anointed One.

FULFILLMENT   c. A.D. 31

Acts 4:25-27 — You spoke by the Holy Spirit through the mouth of your servant, our father David : "'Why do the nations rage and the peoples plot in vain? The kings of the earth take their stand and the rulers gather together against the Lord and against his Anointed One.' Indeed Herod and Pontius Pilate met together with the Gentiles and the people of Israel in this city to conspire against your holy servant Jesus, whom you anointed.

 8. Abandoned by Disciples

PROPHECY   c. 487 B.C.

Zechariah 13:7 — "Awake, O sword, against my shepherd, against the man who is close to me!" declares the LORD Almighty. "Strike the shepherd, and the sheep will be scat-

| 성취 | c. A.D. 31

마태복음 26:31, 56 －『[31] 때에 예수께서 제자들에게 이르시되 오늘 밤에 너희가 다 나를 버리리라 기록된 바 내가 목자를 치리니 양의 떼가 흩어지리라 하였느니라 [56] 그러나 이렇게 된 것은 다 선지자들의 글을 이루려 함이니라 하시더라 이에 제자들이 다 예수를 버리고 도망하니라』

9. 가까운 사람에게 배신당함

| 예언 | c. 970 B.C.

시편 41:9 －『나의 신뢰하는바 내 떡을 먹던 나의 가까운 친구도 나를 대적하여 그 발꿈치를 들었나이다』

| 성취 | c. A.D. 31

요한복음 13:18, 21 －『[18] 내가 너희를 다 가리켜 말하는 것이 아니라 내가 나의 택한 자들이 누구인지 앎이라 그러나 내 떡을 먹는 자가 내게 발꿈치를 들었다 한 성경을 응하게 하려는 것이니라 [21] 예수께서 이 말씀을 하시고 심령에 민망하여 증거하여 가라사대 내가 진실로 진실로 너희에게 이르노니 너희 중 하나가 나를 팔리라 하시니』

tered, and I will turn my hand against the little ones.

FULFILLMENT   c. A.D. 31

Matthew 26:31, 56 — [31] Then Jesus told them, "This very night you will all fall away on account of me, for it is written : "'I will strike the shepherd, and the sheep of the flock will be scattered.' [56] But this has all taken place that the writings of the prophets might be fulfilled." Then all the disciples deserted him and fled.

 ## 9. Betrayed by an Intimidated People

PROPHECY   c. 970 B.C.

Psalms 41:9 — Even my close friend, whom I trusted, he who shared my bread, has lifted up his heel against me.

FULFILLMENT   c. A.D. 31

John 13:18, 21 — [18] "I am not referring to all of you; I know those I have chosen. But this is to fulfill the scripture : 'He who shares my bread has lifted up his heel against me.' [21] After he had said this, Jesus was troubled in spirit and testified, "I tell you the truth, one of you is going to betray me."

🌱 10. 은 30에 팔림

예언 c. 487 B.C.

> 스가랴 11:12 －『내가 그들에게 이르되 너희가 좋게 여기거든 내 고가를 내게 주고 그렇지 아니하거든 말라 그들이 곧 은 삼십을 달아서 내 고가를 삼은지라』

성취 c. A.D. 31

> 마태복음 26:15 －『내가 예수를 너희에게 넘겨 주리니 얼마나 주려느냐 하니 그들이 은 삼십을 달아 주거늘』

10. Sold for 30 Pieces of Silver

PROPHECY c. 487 B.C.

Zechariah 11:12 — I told them, "If you think it best, give me my pay; but if not, keep it." So they paid me thirty pieces of silver.

FULFILLMENT c. A.D. 31

Matthew 26:15 — "and asked, What are you willing to give me if I hand him over to you?" So they counted out for him thirty silver coins.

장 5 범죄자로 고소당함

사 건	예언	역사적 연대	성취	역사적 연대
1. 거짓 증언으로 고소당함	시편 35:11-12	c. 970 B.C.	마가복음 14:57-58	c. A.D. 31
2. 거짓 고소와 비난을 침묵으로 참음	이사야 53:7	c. 690 B.C.	마태복음 26:63	c. A.D. 31

1. 거짓 증언으로 고소당함

예언 c. 970 B.C.

시편 35:11-12 —『불의한 증인이 일어나서 내가 알지 못하는 일로 내게 힐문하며 내게 선을 악으로 갚아 나의 영혼을 외롭게 하나』

성취 c. A.D. 31

마가복음 14:57-58 —『어떤 사람들이 일어나 예수를 쳐서 거짓 증거하여 가로되 우리가 그의 말을 들으니 손으로 지은 이 성전을 내가 헐고 손으로 짓지 아니한 다른 성전을 사흘에 지으리라 하더라 하되』

Chapter 5
Accused of being a Criminal

Event	Prophecy	Chronology	Fulfillment	Chronology
1. Accused by False Witnesses	Psalms 35:11-12	c. 970 B.C.	Mark 14:57-58	c. A.D. 31
2. Perseverance with Silence against False Accusations	Isaiah 53:7	c. 690 B.C.	Matthew 26:63	c. A.D. 31

 1. Accused by False Witnesses

PROPHECY c. 970 B.C.

> **Psalms 35:11-12** — Ruthless witnesses come forward; they question me on things I know nothing about. They repay me evil for good and leave my soul forlorn.

FULFILLMENT c. A.D. 31

> **Mark 14:57-58** — Then some stood up and gave this false testimony against him: "We heard him say, 'I will destroy this man-made temple and in three days will build another, not made by man.'"

2. 거짓 고소와 비난을 침묵으로 참음

예 언   c. 690 B.C.

　이사야 53:7 -『그가 곤욕을 당하여 괴로울 때에도 그 입을 열지 아니하였음이여 마치 도수장으로 끌려가는 어린 양과 털 깎는 자 앞에 잠잠한 양 같이 그 입을 열지 아니하였도다』

성 취   c. A.D. 31

　마태복음 26:63 -『예수께서 잠잠하시거늘 대제사장이 가로되 내가 너로 살아계신 하나님께 맹세하게 하노니 네가 하나님의 아들 그리스도인지 우리에게 말하라』

2. Perseverance with Silence against False Accusations

PROPHECY c. 690 B.C.

> Isaiah 53:7 — He was oppressed and afflicted, yet he did not open his mouth; he was led like a lamb to the slaughter, and as a sheep before her shearers is silent, so he did not open his mouth.

FULFILLMENT c. A.D. 31

> Matthew 26:63 — But Jesus remained silent. The high priest said to him, "I charge you under oath by the living God : Tell us if you are the Christ, the Son of God."

장 6 범죄자로서 십자가에 달림

사 건	예언	역사적 연대	성취	역사적 연대
1. 범죄자로 형벌 받음	이사야 53:12	c. 690 B.C.	마가복음 15:27	c. A.D. 31
2. 저주받고 나무에 달림	신명기 21:23	c. 1410 B.C.	갈라디아서 3:13	c. A.D. 31
3. 놋뱀처럼 십자가에 달림	민수기 21:8-9	c. 1410 B.C.	요한복음 3:14-15	c. A.D. 31
4. 수족이 찔림	시편 22:16	c. 970 B.C.	요한복음 20:25	c. A.D. 31
5. 옆구리가 창으로 찔림	스가랴 12:10	c. 487 B.C.	요한복음 19:34	c. A.D. 31
6. 조롱과 모욕 받음	시편 22:7-8	c. 970 B.C.	마태복음 27:39-44	c. A.D. 31
7. 침 뱉음을 당하고 매맞음	이사야 50:6	c. 690 B.C.	마가복음 14:65	c. A.D. 31
8. 쓸개와 초를 마심	시편 69:21	c. 970 B.C.	마태복음 27:34	c. A.D. 31
9. 겉옷이 제비 뽑힘	시편 22:18	c. 970 B.C.	마태복음 27:35	c. A.D. 31
10. 범죄자를 위해 기도함	시편 109:4 이사야 53:12	c. 970 B.C.	누가복음 23:34	c. A.D. 31
11. 온 세상의 죄를 짐	이사야 53:5, 6, 12	c. 690 B.C.	마태복음 26:28 요한복음 1:29 고린도후서 5:21	c. A.D. 31

1. 범죄자로 형벌 받음

예언 c. 690 B.C.

이사야 53:12 —『이러므로 내가 그로 존귀한 자와 함께 분깃

74 출생 전에 자서전을 쓴 사람(The man who wrote his autobiography before he was born)

Chapter 6
Crucified as a Criminal

Event	Prophecy	Chronology	Fulfillment	Chronology
1. Criminal Punishment	Isaiah 53:12	c. 690 B.C.	Mark 15:27	c. A.D. 31
2. Cursed and Hung on a Tree	Deut. 21:23	c. 1410 B.C.	Galatians 3:13	c. A.D. 31
3. Symbol of the Bronze Snake	Numbers 21:8-9	c. 1410 B.C.	John 3:14-15	c. A.D. 31
4. Pierced Hands and Feet	Psalms 22:16	c. 970 B.C.	John 20:25	c. A.D. 31
5. His Side Pierced with a Spear	Zechariah 12:10	c. 487 B.C.	John 19:34	c. A.D. 31
6. Ridiculed and Insulted	Psalms 22:7-8	c. 970 B.C.	Matthew 27:39-44	c. A.D. 31
7. Struck and Spit on	Isaiah 50:6	c. 690 B.C.	Mark 14:65	c. A.D. 31
8. Drank Gall and Vinegar	Psalms 69:21	c. 970 B.C.	Matthew 27:34	c. A.D. 31
9. Cast Lots for His Garments	Psalms 22:18	c. 970 B.C.	Matthew 27:35	c. A.D. 31
10. Praying for His Persecutors	Psalms 109:4 Isaiah 53:12	c. 970 B.C.	Luke 23:34	c. A.D. 31
11. Bore the Iniquity of the World	Isaiah 53:5, 6, 12	c. 690 B.C.	Matthew 26:28 John 1:29 2 Cor. 5:21	c. A.D. 31

 1. Criminal Punishment

PROPHECY   c. 690 B.C.

Isaiah 53:12 — Therefore I will give him a portion among the

을 얻게 하며 강한 자와 함께 탈취한 것을 나누게 하리니 이는 그가 자기 영혼을 버려 사망에 이르게 하며 범죄자 중 하나로 헤아림을 입었음이라 그러나 실상은 그가 많은 사람의 죄를 지며 범죄자를 위하여 기도하였느니라 하시니라』

성취 c. A.D. 31

마가복음 15:27 -『강도 둘을 예수와 함께 십자가에 못 박으니 하나는 그의 우편에, 하나는 좌편에 있더라』

2. 저주받고 나무에 달림

예언 c. 1410 B.C.

신명기 21:23 -『그 시체를 나무 위에 밤새도록 두지 말고 당일에 장사하여 네 하나님 여호와께서 네게 기업으로 주시는 땅을 더럽히지 말라 나무에 달린 자는 하나님께 저주를 받았음이니라』

성취 c. A.D. 31

갈라디아서 3:13 -『그리스도께서 우리를 위하여 저주를 받은 바 되사 율법의 저주에서 우리를 속량하셨으니 기록된 바 나무에 달린 자마다 저주 아래 있는 자라 하였음이라』

great, and he will divide the spoils with the strong, because he poured out his life unto death, and was numbered with the transgressors. For he bore the sin of many, and made intercession for the transgressors.

FULFILLMENT c. A.D. 31

Mark 15:27 — They crucified two robbers with him, one on his right and one on his left.

 ## 2. Cursed and hung on a tree

PROPHECY c. 1410 B.C.

Deuto. 21:23 — you must not leave his body on the tree overnight. Be sure to bury him that same day, because anyone who is hung on a tree is under God's curse. You must not desecrate the land the LORD your God is giving you as an inheritance.

FULFILLMENT c. A.D. 31

Galatians 3:13 — Christ redeemed us from the curse of the law by becoming a curse for us, for it is written : "Cursed is everyone who is hung on a tree."

3. 놋뱀처럼 십자가에 달림

예언 c. 1410 B.C.

민수기 21:8-9 －『여호와께서 모세에게 이르시되 불뱀을 만들어 장대 위에 달아 물린 자마다 그것을 보면 살리라 모세가 놋뱀을 만들어 장대 위에 다니 뱀에게 물린 자마다 놋뱀을 쳐다본즉 살더라』

성취 c. A.D. 31

요한복음 3:14-15 －『모세가 광야에서 뱀을 든 것 같이 인자도 들려야 하리니 이는 저를 믿는 자마다 영생을 얻게 하려 하심이니라』

4. 수족이 찔림

예언 c. 970 B.C.

시편 22:16 －『개들이 나를 에워쌌으며 악한 무리가 나를 둘러 내 수족을 찔렀나이다』

성취 c. A.D. 31

요한복음 20:25 －『다른 제자들이 그에게 이르되 우리가 주를 보았노라 하니 도마가 가로되 내가 그 손의 못자국을 보며 내 손가락을 그 못자국에 넣으며 내 손을 그 옆구리에 넣

3. Symbol of the Bronze Snake

PROPHECY   c. 1410 B.C.

> Numbers 21:8–9 — The LORD said to Moses, "Make a snake and put it up on a pole; anyone who is bitten can look at it and live." So Moses made a bronze snake and put it up on a pole. Then when anyone was bitten by a snake and looked at the bronze snake, he lived.

FULFILLMENT   c. A.D. 31

> John 3:14–15 — Just as Moses lifted up the snake in the desert, so the Son of Man must be lifted up, that everyone who believes in him may have eternal life.

 ## 4. Pierced Hands and Feet

PROPHECY   c. 970 B.C.

> Psalms 22:16 — Dogs have surrounded me; a band of evil men has encircled me, they have pierced my hands and my feet.

FULFILLMENT   c. A.D. 31

> John 20:25 — So the other disciples told him, "We have seen the Lord!" But he said to them, "Unless I see the nail marks in his hands and put my finger where the nails were, and

어 보지 않고는 믿지 아니하겠노라 하니라』

🌱 5. 옆구리가 창으로 찔림

예언 c. 487 B.C.

스가랴 12:10 －『내가 다윗의 집과 예루살렘 거민에게 은총과 간구하는 심령을 부어 주리니 그들이 그 찌른바 그를 바라보고 그를 위하여 애통하기를 독자를 위하여 애통하듯 하며 그를 위하여 통곡하기를 장자를 위하여 통곡하듯 하리로다』

성취 c. A.D. 31

요한복음 19:34 －『그 중 한 군병이 창으로 옆구리를 찌르니 곧 피와 물이 나오더라』

🌱 6. 조롱과 모욕 받음

예언 c. 970 B.C.

시편 22:7-8 －『나를 보는 자는 다 비웃으며 입술을 비쭉이고 머리를 흔들며 말하되 저가 여호와께 의탁하니 구원하실 걸, 저를 기뻐하시니 건지실 걸 하나이다』

put my hand into his side, I will not believe it."

 5. His Side Pierced with a Spear

PROPHECY   c. 487 B.C.

Zechariah 12:10 — "And I will pour out on the house of David and the inhabitants of Jerusalem a spirit of grace and supplication. They will look on me, the one they have pierced, and they will mourn for him as one mourns for an only child, and grieve bitterly for him as one grieves for a firstborn son.

FULFILLMENT   c. A.D. 31

John 19:34 — Instead, one of the soldiers pierced Jesus' side with a spear, bringing a sudden flow of blood and water.

 6. Ridiculed and Insulted

PROPHECY   c. 970 B.C.

Psalms 22:7–8 — All who see me mock me; they hurl insults, shaking their heads : "He trusts in the LORD; let the LORD rescue him. Let him deliver him, since he delights in him."

성취   c. A.D. 31

마태복음 27:39-44 －『지나가는 자들은 자기 머리를 흔들며 예수를 모욕하여 가로되 성전을 헐고 사흘에 짓는 자여 네가 만일 하나님의 아들이어든 자기를 구원하고 십자가에서 내려오라 하며 그와 같이 대제사장들과 서기관들과 장로들과 함께 희롱하여 가로되 저가 남은 구원하였으되 자기는 구원할 수 없도다 저가 이스라엘의 왕이로다 지금 십자가에서 내려올지어다 그러면 우리가 믿겠노라 저가 하나님을 신뢰하니 하나님이 저를 기뻐하시면 이제 구원하실지라 제 말이 나는 하나님의 아들이라 하였도다 하며 함께 십자가에 못 박힌 강도들도 이와 같이 욕하더라』

7. 침 뱉음을 당하고 매맞음

예언   c. 690 B.C.

이사야 50:6 －『나를 때리는 자들에게 내 등을 맡기며 나의 수염을 뽑는 자들에게 나의 뺨을 맡기며 수욕과 침 뱉음을 피하려고 내 얼굴을 가리우지 아니하였느니라』

성취   c. A.D. 31

마가복음 14:65 －『혹은 그에게 침을 뱉으며 그의 얼굴을 가리우고 주먹으로 치며 가로되 선지자 노릇을 하라 하고 하속들은 손바닥으로 치더라』

FULFILLMENT c. A.D. 31

Matthew 27:39-44 — Those who passed by hurled insults at him, shaking their heads and saying, "You who are going to destroy the temple and build it in three days, save yourself! Come down from the cross, if you are the Son of God!" In the same way the chief priests, the teachers of the law and the elders mocked him. "He saved others," they said, "but he can't save himself! He's the King of Israel! Let him come down now from the cross, and we will believe in him. He trusts in God. Let God rescue him now if he wants him, for he said, 'I am the Son of God.'" In the same way the robbers who were crucified with him also heaped insults on him.

7. Struck and Spit on

PROPHECY c. 690 B.C.

Isaiah 50:6 — I offered my back to those who beat me, my cheeks to those who pulled out my beard; I did not hide my face from mocking and spitting.

FULFILLMENT c. A.D. 31

Mark 14:65 — Then some began to spit at him; they blindfolded him, struck him with their fists, and said, "Prophesy!" And the guards took him and beat him.

🌱 8. 쓸개와 초를 마심

예언   c. 970 B.C.

시편 69:21 —『저희가 쓸개를 나의 식물로 주며 갈할 때에 초로 마시웠사오니』

성취   c. A.D. 31

마태복음 27:34 —『쓸개 탄 포도주를 예수께 주어 마시게 하려 하였더니 예수께서 맛보시고 마시고자 아니하시더라』

🌱 9. 겉옷이 제비 뽑힘

예언   c. 970 B.C.

시편 22:18 —『내 겉옷을 나누며 속옷을 제비뽑나이다』

성취   c. A.D. 31

마태복음 27:35 —『저희가 예수를 십자가에 못 박은 후에 그 옷을 제비 뽑아 나누고』

8. Drank Gall and Vinegar

PROPHECY c. 970 B.C.

> Psalms 69:21 — They put gall in my food and gave me vinegar for my thirst.

FULFILLMENT c. A.D. 31

> Matthew 27:34 — There they offered Jesus wine to drink, mixed with gall; but after tasting it, he refused to drink it.

9. Cast Lots for His Garments

PROPHECY c. 970 B.C.

> Psalms 22:18 — They divide my garments among them and cast lots for my clothing.

FULFILLMENT c. A.D. 31

> Matthew 27:35 — When they had crucified him, they divided up his clothes by casting lots.

10. 범죄자를 위해 기도함

예언 c. 970 B.C.

시편 109:4 – 『나는 사랑하나 저희는 도리어 나를 대적하니 나는 기도할 뿐이라』

이사야 53:12 – 『이러므로 내가 그로 존귀한 자와 함께 분깃을 얻게 하며 강한 자와 함께 탈취한 것을 나누게 하리니 이는 그가 자기 영혼을 버려 사망에 이르게 하며 범죄자 중 하나로 헤아림을 입었음이라 그러나 실상은 그가 많은 사람의 죄를 지며 범죄자를 위하여 기도하였느니라 하시니라』

성취 c. A.D. 31

누가복음 23:34 – 『이에 예수께서 가라사대 아버지여 저희를 사하여 주옵소서 자기의 하는 것을 알지 못함이니이다 하시더라 저희가 그의 옷을 나눠 제비 뽑을새』

11. 온 세상의 죄를 짐

예언 c. 690 B.C.

이사야 53:5, 6, 12 – 『[5] 그가 찔림은 우리의 허물을 인함이요 그가 상함은 우리의 죄악을 인함이라 그가 징계를 받음으로 우리가 평화를 누리고 그가 채찍에 맞음으로 우리가 나음을 입었도다 [6] 우리는 다 양 같아서 그릇 행하여 각기 제

10. Praying for His Persecutors

PROPHECY   c. 970 B.C.

Psalms 109:4 — In return for my friendship they accuse me, but I am a man of prayer.

Isaiah 53:12 — Therefore I will give him a portion among the great, and he will divide the spoils with the strong, because he poured out his life unto death, and was numbered with the transgressors. For he bore the sin of many, and made intercession for the transgressors.

FULFILLMENT   c. A.D. 31

Luke 23:34 — Jesus said, "Father, forgive them, for they do not know what they are doing." And they divided up his clothes by casting lots.

 11. Bore the Iniquity of the World

PROPHECY   c. 690 B.C.

Isaiah 53:5, 6, 12 — [5] But he was pierced for our transgressions, he was crushed for our iniquities; the punishment that brought us peace was upon him, and by his wounds we are healed. [6] We all, like sheep, have gone astray, each

길로 갔거늘 여호와께서는 우리 무리의 죄악을 그에게 담당시키셨도다 [12] 이러므로 내가 그로 존귀한 자와 함께 분깃을 얻게 하며 강한 자와 함께 탈취한 것을 나누게 하리니 이는 그가 자기 영혼을 버려 사망에 이르게 하며 범죄자 중 하나로 헤아림을 입었음이라 그러나 실상은 그가 많은 사람의 죄를 지며 범죄자를 위하여 기도하였느니라 하시니라』

성취
c. A.D. 31

마태복음 26:28 －『이것은 죄 사함을 얻게 하려고 많은 사람을 위하여 흘리는 바 나의 피 곧 언약의 피니라』

요한복음 1:29 －『이튿날 요한이 예수께서 자기에게 나아오심을 보고 가로되 보라 세상 죄를 지고 가는 하나님의 어린 양이로다』

고린도후서 5:21 －『하나님이 죄를 알지도 못하신 자로 우리를 대신하여 죄를 삼으신 것은 우리로 하여금 저의 안에서 하나님의 의가 되게 하려 하심이니라』

of us has turned to his own way; and the LORD has laid on him the iniquity of us all. [12] Therefore I will give him a portion among the great, and he will divide the spoils with the strong, because he poured out his life unto death, and was numbered with the transgressors. For he bore the sin of many, and made intercession for the transgressors.

FULFILLMENT c. A.D. 31

Matthew 26:28 — This is my blood of the covenant, which is poured out for many for the forgiveness of sins.

John 1:29 — The next day John saw Jesus coming toward him and said, "Look, the Lamb of God, who takes away the sin of the world!

2 Cor. 5:21 — God made him who had no sin to be sin for us, so that in him we might become the righteousness of God.

장 7 십자가에서 운명함

사 건	예언	역사적 연대	성취	역사적 연대
1. 하나님께 버림 받음	시편 22:1	c. 915 B.C.	마태복음 27:46	c. A.D. 31
2. 뼈가 하나도 꺾이지 않음	시편 34:20	c. 970 B.C.	요한복음 19:33, 36	c. A.D. 31
3. 예언된 시간에 십자가에서 운명함*	출애굽기 12:6 다니엘 9:25-27	c. 1450 B.C. c. 538 B.C.	마가복음 15:34	c. A.D. 31
4. 죄가 끝남	다니엘 9:24	c. 538 B.C.	요한복음 19:30	c. A.D. 31
5. 부자의 무덤에 장사됨	이사야 53:9	c. 690 B.C.	마태복음 27:57-60	c. A.D. 31

1. 하나님께 버림 받음

예언 c. 915 B.C.

시편 22:1 ―『내 하나님이여 내 하나님이여 어찌 나를 버리셨나이까 어찌 나를 멀리하여 돕지 아니하옵시며 내 신음하는 소리를 듣지 아니하시나이까』

성취 c. A.D. 31

마태복음 27:46 ―『제 구 시 즈음에 예수께서 크게 소리질러 가라사대 엘리 엘리 라마 사박다니 하시니 이는 곧 나의 하나

Chapter 7

Death at the Cross

Event	Prophecy	Chronology	Fulfillment	Chronology
1. Abandoned by God	Psalms 22:1	c. 915 B.C.	Matthew 27:46	c. A.D. 31
2. Not One Bone Broken	Psalms 34:20	c. 970 B.C.	John 19:33, 36	c. A.D. 31
3. Died at the Prophesied Time*	Exodus 12:6 Daniel 9:24-27	c. 1450 B.C. c. 538 B.C.	Mark 15:34	c. A.D. 31
4. Putting an End to Sin	Daniel 9:24	c. 538 B.C.	John 19:30	c. A.D. 31
5. Buried Among the Rich	Isaiah 53:9	c. 690 B.C.	Matthew 27:57-60	c. A.D. 31

 ## 1. Abandoned by God

PROPHECY   c. 915 B.C.

> **Psalms 22:1** — My God, my God, why have you forsaken me? Why are you so far from saving me, so far from the words of my groaning?

FULFILLMENT   c. A.D. 31

> **Matthew 27:46** — About the ninth hour Jesus cried out in a loud voice, "Eloi, Eloi, lama sabachthani?"--which means,

님, 나의 하나님, 어찌하여 나를 버리셨나이까 하는 뜻이라』

2. 뼈가 하나도 꺾이지 않음

예언 c. 970 B.C.

시편 34:20 —『그 모든 뼈를 보호하심이여 그 중에 하나도 꺾이지 아니하도다』

성취 c. A.D. 31

요한복음 19:33, 36 —『[33] 예수께 이르러는 이미 죽은 것을 보고 다리를 꺾지 아니하고 [36] 이 일이 이룬 것은 그 뼈가 하나도 꺾이우지 아니하리라 한 성경을 응하게 하려 함이라』

3. 예언된 시간에 십자가에서 운명함*

예언 c. 1450 B.C. / c. 538 B.C.

출애굽기 12:6 —『이 달 십사일까지 간직하였다가 해질 때에 이스라엘 회중이 그 양을 잡고』

---

*성경은 (다니엘 9:24-27) 약 500년 전에 예수 그리스도의 공생애의 시작뿐만 아니라 죽으심의 사건이 일어날 정확한 시기를 아래와 같이 예언하였다.

"My God, my God, why have you forsaken me?"

 ## 2. Not One Bone Broken

`PROPHECY` c. 970 B.C.

`Psalms 34:20` — he protects all his bones, not one of them will be broken.

`FULFILLMENT` c. A.D. 31

`John 19:33, 36` — [33] But when they came to Jesus and found that he was already dead, they did not break his legs. [36] These things happened so that the scripture would be fulfilled : "Not one of his bones will be broken."

 ## 3. Died at the Prophesied Time*

`PROPHECY` c. 1450 B.C. / c. 538 B.C.

`Exodus 12:6` — Take care of them until the fourteenth day of the month, when all the people of the community of Israel must slaughter them at twilight.

---

* The Bible (Daniel 9:24-27) prophesied around five hundred years beforehand the exact time of the beginning of Jesus' public ministry and also the time of His death.

> 다니엘 9:24-27 -『네 백성과 네 거룩한 성을 위하여 칠십 이레로 기한을 정하였나니 허물이 마치며 죄가 끝나며 죄악이 영속되며 영원한 의가 드러나며 이상과 예언이 응하며 또 지극히 거룩한 자가 기름부음을 받으리라 그러므로 너는 깨달아 알지니라 예루살렘을 중건하라는 영이 날 때부터 기름부음을 받은 자 곧 왕이 일어나기까지 일곱 이레와 육십이 이레가 지날 것이요 그 때 곤란한 동안에 성이 중건되어 거리와 해자가 이룰 것이며 육십이 이레 후에 기름부음을 받은 자가 끊어져 없어질 것이며 장차 한 왕의 백성이 와서 그 성읍과 성소를 훼파하려니와 그의 종말은 홍수에 엄몰됨 같을 것이며 또 끝까지 전쟁이 있으리니 황폐할 것이 작정되었느니라 그가 장차 많은 사람으로 더불어 한 이레 동안의 언약을 굳게 정하겠고 그가 그 이레의 절반에 제사와 예물을 금지할 것이며 또 잔포하여 미운 물건이 날개를 의지하여 설 것이며 또 이미 정한 종말까지 진노가 황폐케 하는 자에게 쏟아지리라 하였느니라』

성취 A.D. 31

> 마가복음 15:34 -『제 구 시에 예수께서 크게 소리지르시되 엘리 엘리 라마 사박다니 하시니 이를 번역하면 나의 하나님 나의 하나님 어찌하여 나를 버리셨나이까 하는 뜻이라』

Daniel 9:24–27 — "Seventy 'sevens' are decreed for your people and your holy city to finish transgression, to put an end to sin, to atone for wickedness, to bring in everlasting righteousness, to seal up vision and prophecy and to anoint the most holy. "Know and understand this : From the issuing of the decree to restore and rebuild Jerusalem until the Anointed One, the ruler, comes, there will be seven 'sevens,' and sixty-two 'sevens.' It will be rebuilt with streets and a trench, but in times of trouble. After the sixty-two 'sevens,' the Anointed One will be cut off and will have nothing. The people of the ruler who will come will destroy the city and the sanctuary. The end will come like a flood : War will continue until the end, and desolations have been decreed. He will confirm a covenant with many for one 'seven.' In the middle of the 'seven' he will put an end to sacrifice and offering. And on a wing of the temple he will set up an abomination that causes desolation, until the end that is decreed is poured out on him."

FULFILLMENT A.D. 31

Mark 15:34 — And at the ninth hour Jesus cried out in a loud voice, "Eloi, Eloi, lama sabachthani?"--which means, "My God, my God, why have you forsaken me?"

70주 예언의 역사적 성취(다니엘 9:24-27)

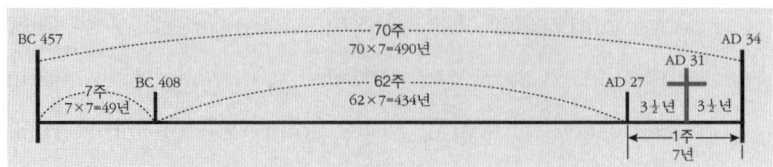

1) "칠십 이레로 기한을 정하였나니"(다니엘 9:24) : 어떤 경우 예언상의 1일은 1년(민수기 14:34; 에스겔 4:6)이므로 70이레 (70주×7일= 490일)는 490년임.
2) "예루살렘을 중건하라는 영이 날 때부터"(다니엘 9:25) : 이는 70주의 예언이 시작되는 해로서 이 칙령이 반포된 해인 기원전 457년에 해당됨. 이 칙령은 페르시아의 아닥사스(Artaxerxes)왕 제7년에 반포되어 주전 457년 가을에 효력이 발생함(에스라 7:8, 12-26, 9:9).
3) "기름 부음을 받은 자"(다니엘 9:25) : 70주의 예언 중에서 62주(434년)가 끝나는 해는 서기 27년으로서 그때 예수는 "성령과 능력을 기름 붓듯 하"(사도행전 10:38)는 침례를 받음으로(누가복음 3:21-22) "기름 부음을 받은 자"를 뜻하는 "메시아"(히브리어), 혹은 "그리스도"(헬라어)로서의 사명을 시작함. "때가 찼다"(마가복음 1:15)라는 예수의 선포는 이 시기에 관한 예언 성취를 언급한 것임.
4) "한 이레 동안"(다니엘 9:27) : 이는 이스라엘을 위하여 할당된 70이레의 마지막 한 주(7년)로서 서기 27년부터 서기 34년에 해당됨. 서기 34년에 스데반이 유대인들에게 순교를 당하므로 이스라엘을 위한 은혜의 시기는 마치고(사도행전 7:51-60) 이방인 시대가 도래 되었음.
5) "육십이 이레 후에 기름 부음을 받은 자가 끊어져 없어질 것"(다니엘 9:26)과 "그 이레의 절반에 제사와 예물을 금지할 것"(다니엘 9:27)은 예수의 죽음을 설명하는 예언임. 이 해는 그가 서기 27년에 메시아로서 공생애를 시작한 후 꼭 한 이레의 절반인 3년 반이 되는 서기 31년임. 이때 성전 휘장이 "위로부터 아래까지 찢어져 둘이"(마태복음 27:51) 되었다. 이는 모든 성전 사역이 폐지되었고 그리스도의 피로 새 언약이 비준됨을(마태복음 26:27-28; 히브리서 10:5-10) 지적하는 것임.
6) 예수 그리스도는 예언된 해인 서기 31년에 십자가에서 운명했을 뿐만 아니라 예언된 시기에 운명하였다. 이스라엘 백성이 출애굽한 후 유대인 달력 정월 10일에 유월절 양이 성별되었다(출애굽기 12:3). 양을 잡는 시간은 정월 14일 늦은 오후 해질녘으로 지정되었다(출애굽기 12:6). 예수는 서기 31년, 오늘날 오후 3시쯤에 해당되는 유대인 달력 정월 14일 제9시쯤(마태복음 27:46)에 십자가에서 운명함으로 그의 죽음에 관한 모든 예언은 성취되었다. 이와 같이 "우리의 유월절 양 곧 그리스도께서 희생이 되셨"(고린도전서 5:7)다.

The Historical Fulfillment of the Seventy Week Prophecy(Daniel 9:24-27)

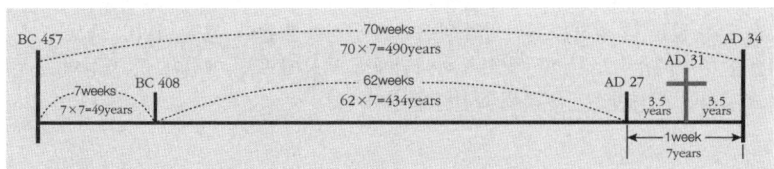

1) "Seventy weeks are determined" (Daniel 9:24): In some Bible prophecy, one day equals one year (Numbers 14:34; Ezekiel 4:6). The seventy weeks therefore represent 490years (70 weeks×7 days = 490 days).
2) "From the going forth of the command to restore and build Jerusalem…" (Daniel 9:25): The year this decree was pronounced was 457 B.C., and corresponds to the beginning of the seventy week prophecy. This decree was promulgated in the seventh year of the King Artaxerxes of Persia and went into effect in the autumn of 457 B.C. (Ezra 7:8, 12-26, 9:9).
3) "The anointed one" (Daniel 9:25): It was in A.D. 27, which corresponded to the ending of the 62 weeks (434 years) in the 70 week prophecy, that Jesus was baptized (Luke 3:21-23). Jesus was anointed with the Holy Spirit and power (Acts 10:38). He began his mission as the Messiah (Hebrew), which means "the anointed" or "Christ" (Greek). In Mark 1:15, Jesus proclaimed that "the time has come," and this referred to the prophecy of Daniel 9:25.
4) "One Week" (Daniel 9:27): This represents the seven years from A.D. 27 through A.D. 34 and is the last week of the seventy weeks assigned to Israel. The martyrdom of Stephen by the Jews in A.D. 34 ended the grace period for Israel (Acts 7:51-60) and began the age of the Gentiles.
5) "After the sixty-two weeks the Messiah shall be cut off" and "in the middle of the week he shall bring an end to sacrifice and offering" (Daniel 9:26, 27): This part of the prophecy refers to Jesus' death. His death occurred in A.D. 31, halfway through the final one week, since Jesus began His ministry as the Messiah in A.D. 27. At that time "the veil of the temple was torn in two from top to bottom" (Matthew 27:51). It signified that the Hebrew Sanctuary ministry was abolished and the new covenant confirmed (Matthew 26:27; Hebrews 10:5-10).
6) Jesus died at the exact hour prophesied: Jesus Christ not only died on the cross in the prophetic year of A.D. 31, but also at the exact time prophesied. After the exodus of the Israelites from Egypt, the Passover lamb was consecrated on the 10th day of the first Jewish month (Exodus 12:3). The lamb was designated to be

*예수 그리스도의 운명의 시기의 예언까지도 유월절 양이 죽임을 당한 시간에 해당되어서 이토록 놀랍게도 정확하게 성취되었다. 누구든지 스스로 믿지 않으려고 일부러 마음을 닫지 않는 한 성경은 하나님의 말씀임을 인정하게 된다. 뿐만 아니라 출생 전에 자서전을 쓴 예수는 오랫동안 예언된, 하나님께서 세상에 보낸 메시아, 즉 세상의 구주라는 역사적이며 객관적인 진리를 확신하게 된다.

🌳 4. 죄가 끝남

예언   c. 538 B.C.

> 다니엘 9:24 — 『네 백성과 네 거룩한 성을 위하여 칠십 이레로 기한을 정하였나니 허물이 마치며 죄가 끝나며 죄악이 영속되며 영원한 의가 드러나며 이상과 예언이 응하며 또 지극히 거룩한 자가 기름부음을 받으리라』

성취   c. A.D. 31

> 요한복음 19:30 — 『예수께서 신 포도주를 받으신 후 가라사대 다 이루었다 하시고 머리를 숙이시고 영혼이 돌아가시니라』

killed on the 14th day at twilight (Exodus 12:6) in the late afternoon. Likewise, Jesus "Christ, our Passover lamb, has been sacrificed" (1 Cor. 5:7). Jesus fulfilled all of the prophecy about his death by his death on the cross on the 14th of the first Jewish month in A.D. 31 about the ninth hour (Matthew 27:46), which corresponds to about 3 pm.

*Amazingly, even the time of Jesus Christ's death was fulfilled exactly, corresponding with the time of the slaying of the Passover lambs. As long as we keep an open mind, we cannot but acknowledge that the Bible is the Word of God. Through confirmation that Jesus died at the very prophetic hour, we are convicted of the objective truth that Jesus, who wrote His autobiography in scripture before He was born, is the Messiah and the Savior of the world sent by God.

4. Putting an End to Sin

`PROPHECY`   c. 538 B.C.

> Daniel 9:24 — "Seventy 'sevens' are decreed for your people and your holy city to finish transgression, to put an end to sin, to atone for wickedness, to bring in everlasting righteousness, to seal up vision and prophecy and to anoint the most holy.

`FULFILLMENT`   c. A.D. 31

> John 19:30 — When he had received the drink, Jesus said, "It is finished." With that, he bowed his head and gave up his spirit.

🌱 5. 부자의 무덤에 장사됨

예언 c. 690 B.C.

이사야 53:9 -『그는 강포를 행치 아니하였고 그 입에 궤사가 없었으나 그 무덤이 악인과 함께 되었으며 그 묘실이 부자와 함께 되었도다』

성취 c. A.D. 31

마태복음 27:57-60 -『저물었을 때에 아리마대 부자 요셉이라 하는 사람이 왔으니 그도 예수의 제자라 빌라도에게 가서 예수의 시체를 달라 하니 이에 빌라도가 내어 주라 분부하거늘 요셉이 시체를 가져다가 정한 세마포로 싸서 바위 속에 판 자기 새 무덤에 넣어두고 큰 돌을 굴려 무덤 문에 놓고 가니』

5. Buried among the Rich

PROPHECY   c. 690 B.C.

Isaiah 53:9 — He was assigned a grave with the wicked, and with the rich in his death, though he had done no violence, nor was any deceit in his mouth.

FULFILLMENT   c. A.D. 31

Matthew 27:57–60 — As evening approached, there came a rich man from Arimathea, named Joseph, who had himself become a disciple of Jesus. Going to Pilate, he asked for Jesus' body, and Pilate ordered that it be given to him. Joseph took the body, wrapped it in a clean linen cloth, and placed it in his own new tomb that he had cut out of the rock. He rolled a big stone in front of the entrance to the tomb and went away.

장 8 부활, 승천하심

사 건	예언	역사적 연대	성취	역사적 연대
1. 부활하심*	시편 16:10, 49:15	c. 960 B.C.	누가복음 24:6, 31, 34 사도행전 13:35	c. A.D. 31
2. 삼일 후에 부활함	요나 1:17	c. 750 B.C.	마태복음 12:39-40 누가복음 24:46	c. A.D. 31
3. 승천하심	시편 68:18, 24:7-10	c. 970 B.C.	마가복음 16:19 에베소서 4:8	c. A.D. 31

1. 부활하심*

예 언 c. 960 B.C.

시편 16:10 —『이는 내 영혼을 음부에 버리지 아니하시며 주의 거룩한 자로 썩지 않게 하실 것임이니이다』

시편 49:15 —『하나님은 나를 영접하시리니 이러므로 내 영혼을 음부의 권세에서 구속하시리로다(셀라)』

---

*예수를 따르는 자들은 예수의 죽음과 부활로 말미암아 하나님을 저들의 하나님이며 저들의 아버지로 주장할 수 있는 권리와 특권을 소유하였다(요한복음 20:17).

Chapter 8
Resurrection & Ascension

Event	Prophecy	Chronology	Fulfillment	Chronology
1. Resurrection*	Psalms 16:10, 49:15	c. 960 B.C.	Luke 24:6, 31, 34 Acts 13:35	c. A.D. 31
2. Resurrection on the Third day	Jonah 1:17	c. 750 B.C.	Matthew 12:39-40 Luke 24:46	c. A.D. 31
3. Ascension	Psalms 68:18, 24:7-10	c. 970 B.C.	Mark 16:19 Ephesians 4:8	c. A.D. 31

 1. Resurrection*

PROPHECY c. 960 B.C.

Psalms 16:10 — because you will not abandon me to the grave, nor will you let your Holy One see decay.

Psalms 49:15 — But God will redeem my life from the grave; he will surely take me to himself. Selah

---

* Through Jesus'death and resurrection, His followers have the right and privilege of claiming God as their God and their Father(John 20:17).

성취   c. A.D. 31

누가복음 24:6, 31, 34 – 『[6] 여기 계시지 않고 살아나셨느니라 갈릴리에 계실 때에 너희에게 어떻게 말씀하신 것을 기억하라 [31] 저희 눈이 밝아져 그인 줄 알아보더니 예수는 저희에게 보이지 아니하시는지라 [34] 말하기를 주께서 과연 살아나시고 시몬에게 나타나셨다 하는지라』

사도행전 13:35 – 『그러므로 또 다른 편에 일렀으되 주의 거룩한 자로 썩음을 당하지 않게 하시리라 하셨느니라』

2. 삼일 후에 부활함

예언   c. 750 B.C.

요나 1:17 – 『여호와께서 이미 큰 물고기를 예비하사 요나를 삼키게 하셨으므로 요나가 삼 일 삼 야를 물고기 배에 있으니라』

성취   c. A.D. 31

마태복음 12:39-40 – 『예수께서 대답하여 가라사대 악하고 음란한 세대가 표적을 구하나 선지자 요나의 표적 밖에는 보일 표적이 없느니라 요나가 밤낮 사흘을 큰 물고기 뱃속에 있었던 것 같이 인자도 밤낮 사흘을 땅 속에 있으리라』

FULFILLMENT c. A.D. 31

Luke 24:6, 31, 34 — [6] He is not here; he has risen! Remember how he told you, while he was still with you in Galilee : [31] Then their eyes were opened and they recognized him, and he disappeared from their sight. [34] and saying, "It is true! The Lord has risen and has appeared to Simon."

Acts 13:35 — So it is stated elsewhere : "'You will not let your Holy One see decay.'

 2. Resurrection after 3 Days

PROPHECY c. 750 B.C.

Jonah 1:17 — But the LORD provided a great fish to swallow Jonah, and Jonah was inside the fish three days and three nights.

FULFILLMENT c. A.D. 31

Matthew 12:39-40 — He answered, "A wicked and adulterous generation asks for a miraculous sign! But none will be given it except the sign of the prophet Jonah. For as Jonah was three days and three nights in the belly of a huge fish, so the Son of Man will be three days and three nights in the heart of the earth.

> 누가복음 24:46 －『또 이르시되 이같이 그리스도가 고난을 받고 제삼일에 죽은 자 가운데서 살아날 것과』

3. 승천하심

예언 c. 970 B.C.

> 시편 68:18 －『주께서 높은 곳으로 오르시며 사로잡은 자를 끌고 선물을 인간에게서, 또는 패역자 중에서 받으시니 여호와 하나님이 저희와 함께 거하려 하심이로다』

> 시편 24:7-10 －『문들아 너희 머리를 들지어다 영원한 문들아 들릴지어다 영광의 왕이 들어가시리로다 영광의 왕이 뉘시뇨 강하고 능한 여호와시요 전쟁에 능한 여호와시로다 문들아 너희 머리를 들지어다 영원한 문들아 들릴지어다 영광의 왕이 들어가시리로다 영광의 왕이 뉘시뇨 만군의 여호와께서 곧 영광의 왕이시로다(셀라)』

성취 c. A.D. 31

> 마가복음 16:19 －『주 예수께서 말씀을 마치신 후에 하늘로 올리우사 하나님 우편에 앉으시니라』

> 에베소서 4:8 －『그러므로 이르기를 그가 위로 올라가실 때에 사로잡힌 자를 사로잡고 사람들에게 선물을 주셨다 하였도다』

Luke 24:46 — He told them, "This is what is written: The Christ will suffer and rise from the dead on the third day.

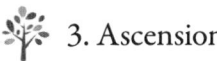
3. Ascension

PROPHECY c. 970 B.C.

Psalms 68:18 — When you ascended on high, you led captives in your train; you received gifts from men, even from the rebellious--that you, O LORD God, might dwell there.

Psalms 24:7–10 — Lift up your heads, O you gates; be lifted up, you ancient doors, that the King of glory may come in. Who is this King of glory? The LORD strong and mighty, the LORD mighty in battle. Lift up your heads, O you gates; lift them up, you ancient doors, that the King of glory may come in. Who is he, this King of glory? The LORD Almighty-- he is the King of glory. Selah

FULFILLMENT c. A.D. 31

Mark 16:19 — After the Lord Jesus had spoken to them, he was taken up into heaven and he sat at the right hand of God.

Ephesians 4:8 — This is why it says : "When he ascended on high, he led captives in his train and gave gifts to men."

장 9 승천 후 하늘에서 봉사함

사 건	예언	역사적 연대	성취	역사적 연대
1. 하나님 보좌 우편에 앉음	시편 110:1	c. 970 B.C.	사도행전 2:34-35	c. A.D. 31
2. 여호와의 아들됨	시편 2:7	c. 970 B.C.	사도행전 13:33	c. A.D. 31
3. 성령의 선물을 교회에 주심	시편 68:18 요엘 2:28-29	c. 970 B.C.	사도행전 2:16-18 에베소서 4:7-8	c. A.D. 31
4. 멜기세덱의 반차를 좇아 영원한 대제사장이 됨	시편 110:4	c. 970 B.C.	히브리서 5:6-10	c. A.D. 31
5. 재림 전 심판을 베풂: 세 천사를 통하여 영원한 복음을 선포함	다니엘 7:9-10, 13-14, 22, 26-27 전도서 12:14 ---- 신약 ---- 마태복음 12:36 사도행전 17:31	c. 538 B.C. c. 935 B.C. c. A.D. 31 c. A.D. 64	요한계시록 14:7	현재

1. 하나님 보좌 우편에 앉음

예언 c. 970 B.C.

시편 110:1 —『여호와께서 내 주에게 말씀하시기를 내가 네 원수로 네 발등상 되게 하기까지 너는 내 우편에 앉으라 하셨도다』

성취 c. A.D. 31

사도행전 2:34-35 —『다윗은 하늘에 올라가지 못하였으나 친히 말하여 가로되 주께서 내 주에게 말씀하시기를 내가 네

Chapter 9
Ministry in Heaven after the Ascension

Event	Prophecy	Chronology	Fulfillment	Chronology
1. To Sit at the Right Hand of God	Psalms 110:1	c. 970 B.C.	Acts 2:34-35	c. A.D. 31
2. Becoming the Son of the Lord	Psalms 2:7	c. 970 B.C.	Acts 13:33	c. A.D. 31
3. Giving Spiritual Gifts to the Church	Psalms 68:18 Joel 2:28-29	c. 970 B.C.	Acts 2:16-18 Ephesians 4:7-8	c. A.D. 31
4. Becoming the Everlasting High Priest in the Order of Melchizedek	Psalms 110:4	c. 970 B.C.	Hebrews 5:6-10	c. A.D. 31
5. Holding the Pre-Advent Judgment and Proclaiming the Everlasting Gospel through the Three Angels	Daniel 7:9-10, 13-14, 22, 26-27 Ecclesiastes 12:14 - New Testament - Matthew 12:36 Acts 17:31	c. 538 B.C. c. 935 B.C. c. A.D. 31 c. A.D. 64	Rev. 14:7	Present

 1. To sit at the Right Hand of God

PROPHECY c. 970 B.C.

Psalms 110:1 — The LORD says to my Lord : "Sit at my right hand until I make your enemies a footstool for your feet."

FULFILLMENT c. A.D. 31

Acts 2:34-35 — For David did not ascend to heaven, and yet he said, "'The Lord said to my Lord : "Sit at my right hand

원수로 네 발등상 되게 하기까지 너는 내 우편에 앉았으라 하셨도다 하였으니』

🌳 2. 여호와의 아들됨

예언 c. 970 B.C.

시편 2:7 -『내가 영을 전하노라 여호와께서 내게 이르시되 너는 내 아들이라 오늘날 내가 너를 낳았도다』

성취 c. A.D. 31

사도행전 13:33 -『곧 하나님이 예수를 일으키사 우리 자녀들에게 이 약속을 이루게 하셨다 함이라 시편 둘째 편에 기록한 바와 같이 너는 내 아들이라 오늘 너를 낳았다 하셨고』

🌳 3. 성령의 선물을 교회에 주심

예언 c. 970 B.C.

시편 68:18 -『주께서 높은 곳으로 오르시며 사로잡은 자를 끌고 선물을 인간에게서, 또는 패역자 중에서 받으시니 여호와 하나님이 저희와 함께 거하려 하심이로다』

요엘 2:28-29 -『그 후에 내가 내 신을 만민에게 부어 주리니 너희 자녀들이 장래일을 말할 것이며 너희 늙은이는 꿈을 꾸

until I make your enemies a footstool for your feet."

2. Becoming the Son of the Lord

PROPHECY c. 970 B.C.

Psalms 2:7 — I will proclaim the decree of the LORD : He said to me, "You are my Son; today I have become your Father.

FULFILLMENT c. A.D. 31

Acts 13:33 — he has fulfilled for us, their children, by raising up Jesus. As it is written in the second Psalm : "'You are my Son; today I have become your Father.'

3. Giving Spiritual Gifts to the Church

PROPHECY c. 970 B.C.

Psalms 68:18 — When you ascended on high, you led captives in your train; you received gifts from men, even from the rebellious--that you, O LORD God, might dwell there.

Joel 2:28-29 — 'And afterward, I will pour out my Spirit on all people. Your sons and daughters will prophesy, your old

며 너희 젊은이는 이상을 볼 것이며 그 때에 내가 또 내 신으로 남종과 여종에게 부어 줄 것이며』

성취 c. A.D. 31

사도행전 2:16-21 ―『이는 곧 선지자 요엘로 말씀하신 것이니 일렀으되 하나님이 가라사대 말세에 내가 내 영으로 모든 육체에게 부어 주리니 너희의 자녀들은 예언할 것이요 너희의 젊은이들은 환상을 보고 너희의 늙은이들은 꿈을 꾸리라 그 때에 내가 내 영으로 내 남종과 여종들에게 부어 주리니 저희가 예언할 것이요 또 내가 위로 하늘에서는 기사와 아래로 땅에서는 징조를 베풀리니 곧 피와 불과 연기로다 주의 크고 영화로운 날이 이르기 전에 해가 변하여 어두워지고 달이 변하여 피가 되리라 누구든지 주의 이름을 부르는 자는 구원을 얻으리라 하였느니라』

에베소서 4:7-8 ―『우리 각 사람에게 그리스도의 선물의 분량대로 은혜를 주셨나니 그러므로 이르기를 그가 위로 올라가실 때에 사로잡힌 자를 사로잡고 사람들에게 선물을 주셨다 하였도다』

men will dream dreams, your young men will see visions. Even on my servants, both men and women, I will pour out my Spirit in those days.

FULFILLMENT c. A.D. 31

Acts 2:16–21 — No, this is what was spoken by the prophet Joel : "'In the last days, God says, I will pour out my Spirit on all people. Your sons and daughters will prophesy, your young men will see visions, your old men will dream dreams. Even on my servants, both men and women, I will pour out my Spirit in those days, and they will prophesy. I will show wonders in the heaven above and signs on the earth below, blood and fire and billows of smoke. The sun will be turned to darkness and the moon to blood before the coming of the great and glorious day of the Lord. And everyone who calls on the name of the Lord will be saved.'

Ephesians 4:7–8 — But to each one of us grace has been given as Christ apportioned it. This is why it says : "When he ascended on high, he led captives in his train and gave gifts to men."

4. 멜기세덱의 반차를 좇아 하늘에서 영원한 대제사장이 됨

예언 c. 970 B.C.

시편 110:4 -『여호와는 맹세하고 변치 아니하시리라 이르시기를 너는 멜기세덱의 반차를 좇아 영원한 제사장이라 하셨도다』

성취 c. A.D. 31

히브리서 5:6-10 -『또한 이와 같이 다른 데 말씀하시되 네가 영원히 멜기세덱의 반차를 좇는 제사장이라 하셨으니 그는 육체에 계실 때에 자기를 죽음에서 능히 구원하실 이에게 심한 통곡과 눈물로 간구와 소원을 올렸고 그의 경외하심을 인하여 들으심을 얻었느니라 그가 아들이시라도 받으신 고난으로 순종함을 배워서 온전하게 되었은즉 자기를 순종하는 모든 자에게 영원한 구원의 근원이 되시고 하나님께 멜기세덱의 반차를 좇은 대제사장이라 칭하심을 받았느니라』

4. Becoming the Everlasting High Priest in the Order of Melchizedek

PROPHECY   c. 970 B.C.

> Psalms 110:4 — The LORD has sworn and will not change his mind : "You are a priest forever, in the order of Melchizedek."

FULFILLMENT   c. A.D. 31

> Hebrews 5:6–10 — And he says in another place, "You are a priest forever, in the order of Melchizedek." During the days of Jesus' life on earth, he offered up prayers and petitions with loud cries and tears to the one who could save him from death, and he was heard because of his reverent submission. Although he was a son, he learned obedience from what he suffered and, once made perfect, he became the source of eternal salvation for all who obey him and was designated by God to be high priest in the order of Melchizedek.

🌳 5. 재림 전 심판을 베풂: 세 천사를 통하여 영원한 복음을 선포함 (현재)

예언 c. 538 B.C.

다니엘 7:9-10, 13-14 — 『[9-10] 내가 보았는데 왕좌가 놓이고 옛적부터 항상 계신 이가 좌정하셨는데 그 옷은 희기가 눈 같고 그 머리털은 깨끗한 양의 털같고 그 보좌는 불꽃이요 그 바퀴는 붙는 불이며 불이 강처럼 흘러 그 앞에서 나오며 그에게 수종하는 자는 천천이요 그 앞에 시위한 자는 만만이며 심판을 베푸는데 책들이 펴 놓였더라 [13-14] 내가 또 밤 이상 중에 보았는데 인자 같은 이가 하늘구름을 타고 와서 옛적부터 항상 계신 자에게 나아와 그 앞에 인도되매 그에게 권세와 영광과 나라를 주고 모든 백성과 나라들과 각 방언하는 자로 그를 섬기게 하였으니 그 권세는 영원한 권세라 옮기지 아니할 것이요 그 나라는 폐하지 아니할 것이니라』

다니엘 7:22, 26-27 — 『[22] 옛적부터 항상 계신 자가 와서 지극히 높으신 자의 성도를 위하여 신원하셨고 때가 이르매 성도가 나라를 얻었더라 [26-27] 그러나 심판이 시작된즉 그는 권세를 빼앗기고 끝까지 멸망할 것이요 나라와 권세와 온 천

5. Holding the Pre-Advent Judgment and Proclaiming the Everlasting Gospel through the Three Angels(Present)

PROPHECY c. 538 B.C.

Daniel 7:9-10, 13-14 — [9-10] As I looked, "thrones were set in place, and the Ancient of Days took his seat. His clothing was as white as snow; the hair of his head was white like wool. His throne was flaming with fire, and its wheels were all ablaze. A river of fire was flowing, coming out from before him. Thousands upon thousands attended him; ten thousand times ten thousand stood before him. The court was seated, and the books were opened. [13-14] "In my vision at night I looked, and there before me was one like a son of man, coming with the clouds of heaven. He approached the Ancient of Days and was led into his presence. He was given authority, glory and sovereign power; all peoples, nations and men of every language worshiped him. His dominion is an everlasting dominion that will not pass away, and his kingdom is one that will never be destroyed.

Daniel 7:22, 26-27 — [22] until the Ancient of Days came and pronounced judgment in favor of the saints of the Most High, and the time came when they possessed the kingdom. [26-27] "'But the court will sit, and his power will be

하 열국의 위세가 지극히 높으신 자의 성민에게 붙인바 되리니 그의 나라는 영원한 나라이라 모든 권세 있는 자가 다 그를 섬겨 복종하리라 하여』

전도서 12:14 -『하나님은 모든 행위와 모든 은밀한 일을 선악간에 심판하시리라』

마태복음 12:36 -『내가 너희에게 이르노니 사람이 무슨 무익한 말을 하든지 심판날에 이에 대하여 심문을 받으리니』

사도행전 17:31 -『이는 정하신 사람으로 하여금 천하를 공의로 심판할 날을 작정하시고 이에 저를 죽은 자 가운데서 다시 살리신 것으로 모든 사람에게 믿을 만한 증거를 주셨음이니라 하니라』

성취 현재

요한계시록 14:7 -『그가 큰 음성으로 가로되 하나님을 두려워하며 그에게 영광을 돌리라 이는 그의 심판하실 시간이 이르렀음이니 하늘과 땅과 바다와 물들의 근원을 만드신 이를 경배하라 하더라』

taken away and completely destroyed forever. Then the sovereignty, power and greatness of the kingdoms under the whole heaven will be handed over to the saints, the people of the Most High. His kingdom will be an everlasting kingdom, and all rulers will worship and obey him.'

Ecclesiastes 12:14 — For God will bring every deed into judgment, including every hidden thing, whether it is good or evil.

Matthew 12:36 — But I tell you that men will have to give account on the day of judgment for every careless word they have spoken.

Acts 17:31 — For he has set a day when he will judge the world with justice by the man he has appointed. He has given proof of this to all men by raising him from the dead."

FULFILLMENT Present

Rev. 14:7 — He said in a loud voice, "Fear God and give him glory, because the hour of his judgment has come. Worship him who made the heavens, the earth, the sea and the springs of water."

장 10 재림 전 마지막 7재앙에서 의인들을 보호하심

〈미래의 사건들〉

사 건	예언	역사적 연대
1. 마지막 7재앙이 예언됨	예레미야 25:29-38 요엘 1:15-20	
2. 세 천사의 기별을 주어 짐승의 표와 하나님의 진노(재림 전 마지막 7재앙)을 받지 않도록 마지막 경고를 발함	요한계시록 14:6-12, 18:1-5	
3. 의인들에게 하나님의 인이 쳐짐	에스겔 9:6 요한계시록 7:1-4	
4. 짐승의 표를 받은 자들에게 부어지는 하나님의 진노	요한계시록 16:1-21	
5. 하나님의 인을 받은 의인들을 7재앙으로부터 보호함	시편 27:5, 46:1-3, 91:3-11 이사야 26:20-21, 33:15-16	

1. 마지막 7재앙이 예언됨

예언

예레미야 25:29-38 ―『보라 내가 내 이름으로 일컬음을 받는 성에서부터 재앙 내리기를 시작하였은즉 너희가 어찌 능히 형벌을 면할 수 있느냐 면치 못하리니 이는 내가 칼을 불러 세상의 모든 거민을 칠 것임이니라 하셨다 하라 만군의 여호와의 말이니라 그러므로 너는 그들에게 이 모든 말로 예언하여 이르기를 여호와께서 높은 데서 부르시며 그 거룩한 처소

Chapter 10
Protecting the Righteous Ones from the Seven Last Plagues before the Second Coming

〈Future Events〉

Event	Prophecy	Chronology
1. The Seven Last Plagues are Predicted	Jeremiah 25:29-38 Joel 1:15-20	
2. Final Warning about the Mark of the Beast and the Wrath of God (the Seven Last Plagues) through giving the Three Angels' Messages	Rev. 14:6-12, 18:1-5	
3. Placing the Seal of God on the Righteous People to protect them from the 7 Plagues	Ezekiel 9:6 Rev. 7:1-4	
4. Wrath of God Poured on those who Received the Mark of the Beast	Rev. 16:1-21	
5. Protecting the Righteous from the Seven Last Plagues	Psalms 27:5, 46:1-3, 91:3-11; Isaiah 26:20-21, 33:15-16	

 1. The Seven Last Plagues are Predicted

PROPHECY

Jeremiah 25:29-38 — See, I am beginning to bring disaster on the city that bears my Name, and will you indeed go unpunished? You will not go unpunished, for I am calling down a sword upon all who live on the earth, declares the LORD Almighty.' "Now prophesy all these words against them and say to them : "'The LORD will roar from on high;

에서 소리를 발하시며 그 양의 우리를 향하여 크게 부르시며 세상 모든 거민을 대하여 포도 밟는 자 같이 외치시리니 요란한 소리가 땅 끝까지 이름은 여호와께서 열국과 다투시며 모든 육체를 심판하시며 악인을 칼에 붙이심을 인함이라 하라 여호와의 말이니라 나 만군의 여호와가 말하노라 보라 재앙이 나서 나라에서 나라에 미칠 것이며 대풍이 땅 끝에서 일어날 것이라 그 날에 나 여호와에게 살륙을 당한 자가 땅 이 끝에서 땅 저 끝에 미칠 것이나 그들이 슬퍼함을 받지 못하며 염습함을 입지 못하며 매장함을 얻지 못하고 지면에서 분토가 되리로다 너희 목자들아 외쳐 애곡하라 너희 양떼의 인도자들아 재에 굴라 이는 너희 도륙을 당할 날과 흩음을 당할 기한이 찼음인즉 너희가 귀한 그릇의 떨어짐 같이 될 것이라 목자들은 도망할 수 없겠고 양떼의 인도자들은 도피할 수 없으리로다 목자들의 부르짖음과 양떼의 인도자들의 애곡하는 소리여 나 여호와가 그들의 초장으로 황폐케 함이로다 평안한 목장들이 적막하니 이는 여호와의 진노의 연고로다 그가 사자 같이 그 소혈에서 나오셨도다 그 잔멸하는 자의 진노와 그 극렬한 분으로 인하여 그들의 땅이 황량하였도다』

요엘 1:15-20 —『오호라 그 날이여 여호와의 날이 가까왔나니 곧 멸망 같이 전능자에게로서 이르리로다 식물이 우리 목

he will thunder from his holy dwelling and roar mightily against his land. He will shout like those who tread the grapes, shout against all who live on the earth. The tumult will resound to the ends of the earth, for the LORD will bring charges against the nations; he will bring judgment on all mankind and put the wicked to the sword,'" declares the LORD. This is what the LORD Almighty says : "Look! Disaster is spreading from nation to nation; a mighty storm is rising from the ends of the earth." At that time those slain by the LORD will be everywhere--from one end of the earth to the other. They will not be mourned or gathered up or buried, but will be like refuse lying on the ground. Weep and wail, you shepherds; roll in the dust, you leaders of the flock. For your time to be slaughtered has come; you will fall and be shattered like fine pottery. The shepherds will have nowhere to flee, the leaders of the flock no place to escape. Hear the cry of the shepherds, the wailing of the leaders of the flock, for the LORD is destroying their pasture. The peaceful meadows will be laid waste because of the fierce anger of the LORD. Like a lion he will leave his lair, and their land will become desolate because of the sword of the oppressor and because of the LORD'S fierce anger.

Joel 1:15–20 — Alas for that day! For the day of the LORD is near; it will come like destruction from the Almighty. Has

전에 끊어지지 아니하였느냐 기쁨과 즐거움이 우리 하나님의 전에 끊어지지 아니하였느냐 씨가 흙덩이 아래서 썩어졌고 창고가 비었고 곳간이 무너졌으니 이는 곡식이 시들었음이로다 생축이 탄식하고 소떼가 민망해하니 이는 꼴이 없음이라 양떼도 피곤하도다 여호와여 내가 주께 부르짖으오니 불이 거친 들의 풀을 살랐고 불꽃이 밭의 모든 나무를 살랐음이니이다 들짐승도 주를 향하여 헐떡거리오니 시내가 다 말랐고 들의 풀이 불에 탔음이니이다』

2. 세 천사의 기별을 주어 짐승의 표와 하나님의 진노 (재림 전 마지막 7재앙)을 받지 않도록 마지막 경고를 발함

예언

요한계시록 14:6-12 —『또 보니 다른 천사가 공중에 날아가는데 땅에 거하는 자들 곧 여러 나라와 족속과 방언과 백성에게 전할 영원한 복음을 가졌더라 그가 큰 음성으로 가로되 하나님을 두려워하며 그에게 영광을 돌리라 이는 그의 심판하실 시간이 이르렀음이니 하늘과 땅과 바다와 물들의 근원을 만드신 이를 경배하라 하더라 또 다른 천사 곧 둘째가 그 뒤를 따라 말하되 무너졌도다 무너졌도다 큰 성 바벨론이여 모든 나라를 그 음행으로 인하여 진노의 포도주로 먹이던 자

not the food been cut off before our very eyes--joy and gladness from the house of our God? The seeds are shriveled beneath the clods. The storehouses are in ruins, the granaries have been broken down, for the grain has dried up. How the cattle moan! The herds mill about because they have no pasture; even the flocks of sheep are suffering. To you, O LORD, I call, for fire has devoured the open pastures and flames have burned up all the trees of the field. Even the wild animals pant for you; the streams of water have dried up and fire has devoured the open pastures.

2. Final Warning about the Mark of the Beast and the Wrath of God(the Seven Last Plagues) through giving the Three Angels' Messages

`PROPHECY`

Rev. 14:6–12 — Then I saw another angel flying in midair, and he had the eternal gospel to proclaim to those who live on the earth--to every nation, tribe, language and people. He said in a loud voice, "Fear God and give him glory, because the hour of his judgment has come. Worship him who made the heavens, the earth, the sea and the springs of water." A second angel followed and said, "Fallen! Fallen is Babylon the Great, which made all the nations drink the maddening

로다 하더라 또 다른 천사 곧 셋째가 그 뒤를 따라 큰 음성으로 가로되 만일 누구든지 짐승과 그의 우상에게 경배하고 이마에나 손에 표를 받으면 그도 하나님의 진노의 포도주를 마시리니 그 진노의 잔에 섞인 것이 없이 부은 포도주라 거룩한 천사들 앞과 어린 양 앞에서 불과 유황으로 고난을 받으리니 그 고난의 연기가 세세토록 올라가리로다 짐승과 그의 우상에게 경배하고 그 이름의 표를 받는 자는 누구든지 밤낮 쉼을 얻지 못하리라 하더라 성도들의 인내가 여기 있나니 저희는 하나님의 계명과 예수 믿음을 지키는 자니라』

요한계시록 18:1-5 －『이 일 후에 다른 천사가 하늘에서 내려오는 것을 보니 큰 권세를 가졌는데 그의 영광으로 땅이 환하여지더라 힘센 음성으로 외쳐 가로되 무너졌도다 무너졌도다 큰 성 바벨론이여 귀신의 처소와 각종 더러운 영의 모이는 곳과 각종 더럽고 가증한 새의 모이는 곳이 되었도다 그 음행의 진노의 포도주를 인하여 만국이 무너졌으며 또 땅의 왕들이 그로 더불어 음행하였으며 땅의 상고들도 그 사치의 세력을 인하여 치부하였도다 하더라 또 내가 들으니 하늘로서 다른 음성이 나서 가로되 내 백성아, 거기서 나와 그의 죄에 참예하지 말고 그의 받을 재앙들을 받지 말라 그 죄는 하늘에 사무쳤으며 하나님은 그의 불의한 일을 기억하신지라』

wine of her adulteries." A third angel followed them and said in a loud voice : "If anyone worships the beast and his image and receives his mark on the forehead or on the hand, he, too, will drink of the wine of God's fury, which has been poured full strength into the cup of his wrath. He will be tormented with burning sulfur in the presence of the holy angels and of the Lamb. And the smoke of their torment rises for ever and ever. There is no rest day or night for those who worship the beast and his image, or for anyone who receives the mark of his name." This calls for patient endurance on the part of the saints who obey God's commandments and remain faithful to Jesus.

Rev 18:1-5 — After this I saw another angel coming down from heaven. He had great authority, and the earth was illuminated by his splendor. With a mighty voice he shouted : "Fallen! Fallen is Babylon the Great! She has become a home for demons and a haunt for every evil spirit, a haunt for every unclean and detestable bird. For all the nations have drunk the maddening wine of her adulteries. The kings of the earth committed adultery with her, and the merchants of the earth grew rich from her excessive luxuries." Then I heard another voice from heaven say : "Come out of her, my people, so that you will not share in her sins, so that you will not receive any of her plagues; for her sins are piled up

3. 의인들에게 하나님의 인이 쳐짐

예언

에스겔 9:6 -『늙은 자와 젊은 자와 처녀와 어린 아이와 부녀를 다 죽이되 이마에 표 있는 자에게는 가까이 말라 내 성소에서 시작할지니라 하시매 그들이 성전 앞에 있는 늙은 자들로부터 시작하더라』

요한계시록 7:1-4 -『이 일 후에 내가 네 천사가 땅 네 모퉁이에 선 것을 보니 땅의 사방의 바람을 붙잡아 바람으로 하여금 땅에나 바다에나 각종 나무에 불지 못하게 하더라 또 보매 다른 천사가 살아 계신 하나님의 인을 가지고 해 돋는 데로부터 올라와서 땅과 바다를 해롭게 할 권세를 얻은 네 천사를 향하여 큰 소리로 외쳐 가로되 우리가 우리 하나님의 종들의 이마에 인치기까지 땅이나 바다나 나무나 해하지 말라 하더라 내가 인 맞은 자의 수를 들으니 이스라엘 자손의 각 지파 중에서 인 맞은 자들이 십사만 사천이니』

to heaven, and God has remembered her crimes.

3. Placing the Seal of God on the Righteous People to protect them from the 7 Plagues

`PROPHECY`

`Ezekiel 9:6` — Slaughter old men, young men and maidens, women and children, but do not touch anyone who has the mark. Begin at my sanctuary." So they began with the elders who were in front of the temple.

`Rev. 7:1–4` — After this I saw four angels standing at the four corners of the earth, holding back the four winds of the earth to prevent any wind from blowing on the land or on the sea or on any tree. Then I saw another angel coming up from the east, having the seal of the living God. He called out in a loud voice to the four angels who had been given power to harm the land and the sea: "Do not harm the land or the sea or the trees until we put a seal on the foreheads of the servants of our God." Then I heard the number of those who were sealed: 144,000 from all the tribes of Israel.

4. 짐승의 표를 받은 자들에게 부어지는 하나님의 진노

> 예언

*요한계시록 16:1-21 - 『또 내가 들으니 성전에서 큰 음성이 나서 일곱 천사에게 말하되 너희는 가서 하나님의 진노의 일곱 대접을 땅에 쏟으라 하더라 첫째가 가서 그 대접을 땅에 쏟으며 악하고 독한 헌데가 짐승의 표를 받은 사람들과 그 우상에게 경배하는 자들에게 나더라 둘째가 그 대접을 바다에 쏟으매 바다가 곧 죽은 자의 피 같이 되니 바다 가운데 모든 생물이 죽더라 셋째가 그 대접을 강과 물 근원에 쏟으매 피가 되더라 내가 들으니 물을 차지한 천사가 가로되 전에도 계셨고 시방도 계신 거룩하신 이여 이렇게 심판하시니 의로우시도다 저희가 성도들과 선지자들의 피를 흘렸으므로 저희로 피를 마시게 하신 것이 합당하니이다 하더라 또 내가 들으니 제단이 말하기를 그러하다 주 하나님 곧 전능하신 이시여 심판하시는 것이 참되시고 의로우시도다 하더라 넷째가 그 대접을 해에 쏟으매 해가 권세를 받아 불로 사람들을 태우니 사람들이 크게 태움에 태워진지라 이 재앙들을 행하는 권세를 가지신 하나님의 이름을 훼방하며 또 회개하여 영광을 주께 돌리지 아니하더라 또 다섯째가 그 대접을 짐승의 보좌에 쏟으니 그 나라가 곧 어두워지며 사람들이 아파서 자기 혀를 깨물고 아픈 것과 종기로 인하여 하늘의 하나님을 훼방하고 저희 행위를 회개치 아니하더라 또 여섯째가 그 대접을 큰 강 유브라데에 쏟으매 강물이 말라서 동방에서 오는

4. Wrath of God Poured on those who Received the Mark of the Beast

PROPHECY

Rev. 16:1–21 — Then I heard a loud voice from the temple saying to the seven angels, "Go, pour out the seven bowls of God's wrath on the earth." The first angel went and poured out his bowl on the land, and ugly and painful sores broke out on the people who had the mark of the beast and worshiped his image. The second angel poured out his bowl on the sea, and it turned into blood like that of a dead man, and every living thing in the sea died. The third angel poured out his bowl on the rivers and springs of water, and they became blood. Then I heard the angel in charge of the waters say : "You are just in these judgments, you who are and who were, the Holy One, because you have so judged; for they have shed the blood of your saints and prophets, and you have given them blood to drink as they deserve." And I heard the altar respond : "Yes, Lord God Almighty, true and just are your judgments." The fourth angel poured out his bowl on the sun, and the sun was given power to scorch people with fire. They were seared by the intense heat and they cursed the name of God, who had control over these plagues, but they refused to repent and glorify him. The fifth angel poured out his bowl on the throne

왕들의 길이 예비되더라 또 내가 보매 개구리 같은 세 더러운 영이 용의 입과 짐승의 입과 거짓 선지자의 입에서 나오니 저희는 귀신의 영이라 이적을 행하여 온 천하 임금들에게 가서 하나님 곧 전능하신 이의 큰 날에 전쟁을 위하여 그들을 모으더라 보라 내가 도적 같이 오리니 누구든지 깨어 자기 옷을 지켜 벌거벗고 다니지 아니하며 자기의 부끄러움을 보이지 아니하는 자가 복이 있도다 세 영이 히브리 음으로 아마겟돈이라 하는 곳으로 왕들을 모으더라 일곱째가 그 대접을 공기 가운데 쏟으매 큰 음성이 성전에서 보좌로부터 나서 가로되 되었다 하니 번개와 음성들과 뇌성이 있고 또 지진이 있어 어찌 큰지 사람이 땅에 있어 옴으로 이같이 큰 지진이 없었더라 큰 성이 세 갈래로 갈라지고 만국의 성들도 무너지니 큰 성 바벨론이 하나님 앞에 기억하신 바 되어 그의 맹렬한 진노의 포도주 잔을 받으매 각 섬도 없어지고 산악도 간데 없더라 또 중수가 한 달란트나 되는 큰 우박이 하늘로부터 사람들에게 내리매 사람들이 그 박재로 인하여 하나님을 훼방하니 그 재앙이 심히 큼이러라』

of the beast, and his kingdom was plunged into darkness. Men gnawed their tongues in agony and cursed the God of heaven because of their pains and their sores, but they refused to repent of what they had done. The sixth angel poured out his bowl on the great river Euphrates, and its water was dried up to prepare the way for the kings from the East. Then I saw three evil spirits that looked like frogs; they came out of the mouth of the dragon, out of the mouth of the beast and out of the mouth of the false prophet. They are spirits of demons performing miraculous signs, and they go out to the kings of the whole world, to gather them for the battle on the great day of God Almighty. "Behold, I come like a thief! Blessed is he who stays awake and keeps his clothes with him, so that he may not go naked and be shamefully exposed." Then they gathered the kings together to the place that in Hebrew is called Armageddon. The seventh angel poured out his bowl into the air, and out of the temple came a loud voice from the throne, saying, "It is done!" Then there came flashes of lightning, rumblings, peals of thunder and a severe earthquake. No earthquake like it has ever occurred since man has been on earth, so tremendous was the quake. The great city split into three parts, and the cities of the nations collapsed. God remembered Babylon the Great and gave her the cup filled with the wine of the fury of his wrath. Every island fled away

5. 하나님의 인을 받은 의인들을 7재앙으로부터 보호함

예언

시편 27:5 -『여호와께서 환난 날에 나를 그 초막 속에 비밀히 지키시고 그 장막 은밀한 곳에 나를 숨기시며 바위 위에 높이 두시리로다』

시편 46:1-3 -『하나님은 우리의 피난처시요 힘이시니 환난 중에 만날 큰 도움이시라 그러므로 땅이 변하든지 산이 흔들려 바다 가운데 빠지든지 바닷물이 흉용하고 뛰놀든지 그것이 넘침으로 산이 요동할지라도 우리는 두려워 아니하리로다(셀라)』

시편 91:3-11 -『이는 저가 너를 새 사냥꾼의 올무에서와 극한 염병에서 건지실 것임이로다 저가 너를 그 깃으로 덮으시리니 네가 그 날개 아래 피하리로다 그의 진실함은 방패와 손 방패가 되나니 너는 밤에 놀램과 낮에 흐르는 살과 흑암 중에 행하는 염병과 백주에 황폐케 하는 파멸을 두려워 아니하리로다 천 인이 네 곁에서, 만인이 네 우편에서 엎드러지나

and the mountains could not be found. From the sky huge hailstones of about a hundred pounds each fell upon men. And they cursed God on account of the plague of hail, because the plague was so terrible.

5. Protecting the Righteous from the Seven Last Plagues

PROPHECY

Psalms 27:5 — For in the day of trouble he will keep me safe in his dwelling; he will hide me in the shelter of his tabernacle and set me high upon a rock.

Psalms 46:1–3 — God is our refuge and strength, an ever-present help in trouble. Therefore we will not fear, though the earth give way and the mountains fall into the heart of the sea, though its waters roar and foam and the mountains quake with their surging. Selah

Psalms 91:3–11 — Surely he will save you from the fowler's snare and from the deadly pestilence. He will cover you with his feathers, and under his wings you will find refuge; his faithfulness will be your shield and rampart. You will not fear the terror of night, nor the arrow that flies by day, nor the pestilence that stalks in the darkness, nor the

이 재앙이 네게 가까이 못하리로다 오직 너는 목도하리니 악인의 보응이 네게 보이리로다 네가 말하기를 여호와는 나의 피난처시라 하고 지존자로 거처를 삼았으므로 화가 네게 미치지 못하며 재앙이 네 장막에 가까이 오지 못하리니 저가 너를 위하여 그 사자들을 명하사 네 모든 길에 너를 지키게 하심이라』

이사야 26:20-21 -『내 백성아 갈지어다 네 밀실에 들어가서 네 문을 닫고 분노가 지나기까지 잠간 숨을지어다 보라 여호와께서 그 처소에서 나오사 땅의 거민의 죄악을 벌하실 것이라 땅이 그 위에 잦았던 피를 드러내고 그 살해당한 자를 다시는 가리우지 아니하리라』

이사야 33:15-16 -『오직 의롭게 행하는 자, 정직히 말하는자, 토색한 재물을 가증히 여기는 자, 손을 흔들어 뇌물을 받지 아니하는 자, 귀를 막아 피 흘리려는 꾀를 듣지 아니하는 자, 눈을 감아 악을 보지 아니하는 자, 그는 높은 곳에 거하리니 견고한 바위가 그 보장이 되며 그 양식은 공급되고 그 물은 끊치지 아니하리라 하셨느니라』

plague that destroys at midday. A thousand may fall at your side, ten thousand at your right hand, but it will not come near you. You will only observe with your eyes and see the punishment of the wicked. If you make the Most High your dwelling--even the LORD, who is my refuge-- then no harm will befall you, no disaster will come near your tent. For he will command his angels concerning you to guard you in all your ways;

Isaiah 26:20-21 — Go, my people, enter your rooms and shut the doors behind you; hide yourselves for a little while until his wrath has passed by. See, the LORD is coming out of his dwelling to punish the people of the earth for their sins. The earth will disclose the blood shed upon her; she will conceal her slain no longer.

Isaiah 33:15-16 — He who walks righteously and speaks what is right, who rejects gain from extortion and keeps his hand from accepting bribes, who stops his ears against plots of murder and shuts his eyes against contemplating evil-- this is the man who will dwell on the heights, whose refuge will be the mountain fortress. His bread will be supplied, and water will not fail him.

장 11 세상에 다시 강림함(재림)

사 건	예언		역사적 연대
A. 출생 전 예언함	1. 에녹을 통해	유다서 1:14	
	2. 욥을 통해	욥기 19:25-26	
	3. 시편 기자를 통해	시편 50:3-6, 102:15-16	
	4. 이사야를 통해	이사야 25:9, 40:10	
	5. 호세아를 통해	호세아 13:14	
	6. 미가를 통해	미가 1:3-4	
B. 승천하기 전 제자들에게 예언함	1. 마태를 통해	마태복음 24:30-31, 26:64	
	2. 누가를 통해	누가복음 9:26	
	3. 요한을 통해	요한복음 14:1-3	
C. 승천시 예언함	천사를 통해	사도행전 1:11	
D. 승천 후 예언함	1. 베드로를 통해	베드로전서 1:7, 5:4 베드로후서 3:9-10	
	2. 바울을 통해	고린도전서 15:50-57 골로새서 3:4 데살로니가전서 4:13-17 데살로니가후서 1:7-10, 2:8 디모데전서 6:14 히브리서 9:28, 10:37	
	3. 요한을 통해	요한1서 2:28, 3:2 요한계시록 1:7, 19:11-21, 22:20	

138 출생 전에 자서전을 쓴 사람(The man who wrote his autobiography before he was born)

Chapter 11 Returning to Earth: The Second Coming

Event	Prophecy		Chronology
1. Prophesied before His Birth	-through Enoch	Jude 1:14	
	-through Job	Job 19:25-26	
	-through David	Psalms 50:3-6, 102:15-16	
	-through Isaiah	Isaiah 25:9, 40:10	
	-through Hosea	Hosea 13:14	
	-through Micah	Micah 1:3-4	
2. Prophesied to the Disciples before His Ascension	-through Matthew	Matthew 24:30-31, 26:64	
	-through Luke	Luke 9:26	
	-through John	John 14:1-3	
3. Prophesied at the Ascension	-through the Angel	Acts 1:11	
4. Prophesied after the Ascension	-through Peter	1 Peter 1:7, 5:4 2 Peter 3:9-10	
	-through Paul	1 Corinthians 15:50-57 Colossians 3:4 1 Thessalonians 4:13-17 2 Thessalonians 1:7-10, 2:8 1 Timothy 6:14 Hebrews 9:28, 10:37	
	-through John	1 John 2:28, 3:2 Revelation 1:7, 19:11-21, 22:20	

1. 출생 전 예언함

- **에녹을 통해**

  유다서 1:14 - 『아담의 칠세 손 에녹이 사람들에게 대하여도 예언하여 이르되 보라 주께서 그 수만의 거룩한 자와 함께 임하셨나니』

- **욥을 통해**

  욥기 19:25-26 - 『내가 알기에는 나의 구속자가 살아 계시니 후일에 그가 땅 위에 서실 것이라 나의 이 가죽, 이것이 썩은 후에 내가 육체 밖에서 하나님을 보리라』

- **시편 기자를 통해**

  시편 50:3-6 - 『우리 하나님이 임하사 잠잠치 아니하시니 그 앞에는 불이 삼키고 그 사방에는 광풍이 불리로다 하나님이 그 백성을 판단하시려고 윗 하늘과 아래 땅에 반포하여 이르시되 나의 성도를 내 앞에 모으라 곧 제사로 나와 언약한 자니라 하시도다』

  시편 102:15-16 - 『이에 열방이 여호와의 이름을 경외하며 세계 열왕이 주의 영광을 경외하리니 대저 여호와께서 시온을 건설하시고 그 영광 중에 나타나셨음이라』

1. Prophesied before His Birth

― through Enoch

Jude 1:14 ― Enoch, the seventh from Adam, prophesied about these men : "See, the Lord is coming with thousands upon thousands of his holy ones

― through Job

Job 19:25–26 ― I know that my Redeemer lives, and that in the end he will stand upon the earth. And after my skin has been destroyed, yet in my flesh I will see God;

― through David

Psalms 50:3–6 ― Our God comes and will not be silent; a fire devours before him, and around him a tempest rages. He summons the heavens above, and the earth, that he may judge his people : "Gather to me my consecrated ones, who made a covenant with me by sacrifice." And the heavens proclaim his righteousness, for God himself is judge. Selah

Psalms 102:15–16 ― The nations will fear the name of the LORD, all the kings of the earth will revere your glory. For the LORD will rebuild Zion and appear in his glory.

- 이사야를 통해

　　이사야 25:9 －『그 날에 말하기를 이는 우리의 하나님이시라 우리가 그를 기다렸으니 그가 우리를 구원하시리로다 이는 여호와시라 우리가 그를 기다렸으니 우리는 그 구원을 기뻐하며 즐거워하리라 할 것이며』

　　이사야 40:10 －『보라 주 여호와께서 장차 강한 자로 임하실 것이요 친히 그 팔로 다스리실 것이라 보라 상급이 그에게 있고 보응이 그 앞에 있으며』

- 호세아를 통해

　　호세아 13:14 －『내가 저희를 음부의 권세에서 속량하며 사망에서 구속하리니 사망아 네 재앙이 어디 있느냐 음부야 네 멸망이 어디 있느냐 뉘우침이 내 목전에 숨으리라』

- 미가를 통해

　　미가 1:3-4 －『여호와께서 그 처소에서 나오시고 강림하사 땅의 높은 곳을 밟으실 것이라 그 아래서 산들이 녹고 골짜기들이 갈라지기를 불 앞의 밀 같고 비탈로 쏟아지는 물 같을 것이니』

- through Isaiah

    Isaiah 25:9 — In that day they will say, "Surely this is our God; we trusted in him, and he saved us. This is the LORD, we trusted in him; let us rejoice and be glad in his salvation."

    Isaiah 40:10 — See, the Sovereign LORD comes with power, and his arm rules for him. See, his reward is with him, and his recompense accompanies him.

- through Hosea

    Hosea 13:14 — I will ransom them from the power of the grave ; I will redeem them from death. Where, O death, are your plagues? Where, O grave, is your destruction? "I will have no compassion,

- through Micah

    Micah 1:3-4 — Look! The LORD is coming from his dwelling place; he comes down and treads the high places of the earth. The mountains melt beneath him and the valleys split apart, like wax before the fire, like water rushing down a slope.

2. 승천하기 전 제자들에게 예언함

- 마태를 통해

마태복음 24:30-31 - 『그 때에 인자의 징조가 하늘에서 보이겠고 그 때에 땅의 모든 족속들이 통곡하며 그들이 인자가 구름을 타고 능력과 큰 영광으로 오는 것을 보리라 저가 큰 나팔 소리와 함께 천사들을 보내리니 저희가 그 택하신 자들을 하늘 이 끝에서 저 끝까지 사방에서 모으리라』

마태복음 26:64 - 『예수께서 가라사대 네가 말하였느니라 그러나 내가 너희에게 이르노니 이 후에 인자가 권능의 우편에 앉은 것과 하늘 구름을 타고 오는 것을 너희가 보리라 하시니』

- 누가를 통해

누가복음 9:26 - 『누구든지 나와 내 말을 부끄러워하면 인자도 자기와 아버지와 거룩한 천사들의 영광으로 올 때에 그 사람을 부끄러워하리라』

- 요한을 통해

요한복음 14:1-3 - 『너희는 마음에 근심하지 말라 하나님을 믿으니 또 나를 믿으라 내 아버지 집에 거할 곳이 많도다 그렇지 않으면 너희에게 일렀으리라 내가 너희를 위하여 처소

2. Prophesied to the Disciples before His Ascension

― through Matthew

Matthew 24:30–31 ― "At that time the sign of the Son of Man will appear in the sky, and all the nations of the earth will mourn. They will see the Son of Man coming on the clouds of the sky, with power and great glory. And he will send his angels with a loud trumpet call, and they will gather his elect from the four winds, from one end of the heavens to the other.

Matthew 26:64 ― "Yes, it is as you say," Jesus replied. "But I say to all of you : In the future you will see the Son of Man sitting at the right hand of the Mighty One and coming on the clouds of heaven."

― through Luke

Luke 9:26 ― If anyone is ashamed of me and my words, the Son of Man will be ashamed of him when he comes in his glory and in the glory of the Father and of the holy angels.

― through John

John 14:1–3 ― "Do not let your hearts be troubled. Trust in God; trust also in me. In my Father's house are many rooms; if it were not so, I would have told you. I am going there to

를 예비하러 가노니 가서 너희를 위하여 처소를 예비하면 내가 다시 와서 너희를 내게로 영접하여 나 있는 곳에 너희도 있게 하리라』

3. 승천시 예언함

- 천사를 통해

사도행전 1:11 -『가로되 갈릴리 사람들아 어찌하여 서서 하늘을 쳐다보느냐 너희 가운데서 하늘로 올리우신 이 예수는 하늘로 가심을 본 그대로 오시리라 하였느니라』

4. 승천 후 예언함

- 베드로를 통해

베드로전서 1:7 -『너희 믿음의 시련이 불로 연단하여도 없어질 금보다 더 귀하여 예수 그리스도의 나타나실 때에 칭찬과 영광과 존귀를 얻게 하려 함이라』

베드로전서 5:4 -『그리하면 목자장이 나타나실 때에 시들지 아니하는 영광의 면류관을 얻으리라』

prepare a place for you. And if I go and prepare a place for you, I will come back and take you to be with me that you also may be where I am.

 ## 3. Prophesied at the Ascension

― through the Angel

Acts 1:11 ― "Men of Galilee," they said, "why do you stand here looking into the sky? This same Jesus, who has been taken from you into heaven, will come back in the same way you have seen him go into heaven."

 ## 4. After the Ascension

― through Peter

1 Peter 1:7 ― These have come so that your faith--of greater worth than gold, which perishes even though refined by fire--may be proved genuine and may result in praise, glory and honor when Jesus Christ is revealed.

1 Peter 5:4 ― And when the Chief Shepherd appears, you will receive the crown of glory that will never fade away.

베드로후서 3:9-10 -『주의 약속은 어떤 이의 더디다고 생각하는 것 같이 더딘 것이 아니라 오직 너희를 대하여 오래 참으사 아무도 멸망치 않고 다 회개하기에 이르기를 원하시느니라 그러나 주의 날이 도적 같이 오리니 그 날에는 하늘이 큰 소리로 떠나가고 체질이 뜨거운 불에 풀어지고 땅과 그 중에 있는 모든 일이 드러나리로다』

- **바울을 통해**

고린도전서 15:50-57 -『형제들아 내가 이것을 말하노니 혈과 육은 하나님 나라를 유업으로 받을 수 없고 또한 썩은 것은 썩지 아니한 것을 유업으로 받지 못하느니라 보라 내가 너희에게 비밀을 말하노니 우리가 다 잠잘 것이 아니요 마지막 나팔에 순식간에 홀연히 다 변화하리니 나팔 소리가 나매 죽은 자들이 썩지 아니할 것으로 다시 살고 우리도 변화하리라 이 썩을 것이 불가불 썩지 아니할 것을 입겠고 이 죽을 것이 죽지 아니함을 입으리로다 이 썩을 것이 썩지 아니함을 입고 이 죽을 것이 죽지 아니함을 입을 때에는 사망이 이김의 삼킨 바 되리라고 기록된 말씀이 응하리라 사망아 너의 이기는 것이 어디 있느냐 사망아 너의 쏘는 것이 어디 있느냐 사망의 쏘는 것은 죄요 죄의 권능은 율법이라 우리 주 예수 그리스도로 말미암아 우리에게 이김을 주시는 하나님께 감사하노니』

골로새서 3:4 -『우리 생명이신 그리스도께서 나타나실 그 때

2 Peter 3:9-10 — The Lord is not slow in keeping his promise, as some understand slowness. He is patient with you, not wanting anyone to perish, but everyone to come to repentance. But the day of the Lord will come like a thief. The heavens will disappear with a roar; the elements will be destroyed by fire, and the earth and everything in it will be laid bare.

— through Paul

1 Corinthians 15:50-57 — I declare to you, brothers, that flesh and blood cannot inherit the kingdom of God, nor does the perishable inherit the imperishable. Listen, I tell you a mystery : We will not all sleep, but we will all be changed-- in a flash, in the twinkling of an eye, at the last trumpet. For the trumpet will sound, the dead will be raised imperishable, and we will be changed. For the perishable must clothe itself with the imperishable, and the mortal with immortality. When the perishable has been clothed with the imperishable, and the mortal with immortality, then the saying that is written will come true : "Death has been swallowed up in victory." "Where, O death, is your victory? Where, O death, is your sting?" The sting of death is sin, and the power of sin is the law. But thanks be to God! He gives us the victory through our Lord Jesus Christ.

Colossians 3:4 — When Christ, who is your life, appears,

에 너희도 그와 함께 영광 중에 나타나리라』

데살로니가전서 4:13-17 - 『형제들아 자는 자들에 관하여는 너희가 알지 못함을 우리가 원치 아니하노니 이는 소망 없는 다른 이와 같이 슬퍼하지 않게 하려 함이라 우리가 예수의 죽었다가 다시 사심을 믿을진대 이와 같이 예수 안에서 자는 자들도 하나님이 저와 함께 데리고 오시리라 우리가 주의 말씀으로 너희에게 이것을 말하노니 주 강림하실 때까지 우리 살아 남아 있는 자도 자는 자보다 결단코 앞서지 못하리라 주께서 호령과 천사장의 소리와 하나님의 나팔로 친히 하늘로 좇아 강림하시리니 그리스도 안에서 죽은 자들이 먼저 일어나고 그 후에 우리 살아 남은 자도 저희와 함께 구름 속으로 끌어올려 공중에서 주를 영접하게 하시리니 그리하여 우리가 항상 주와 함께 있으리라』

데살로니가후서 1:7-10 - 『환난 받는 너희에게는 우리와 함께 안식으로 갚으시는 것이 하나님의 공의시니 주 예수께서 저의 능력의 천사들과 함께 하늘로부터 불꽃 중에 나타나실 때에 하나님을 모르는 자들과 우리 주 예수의 복음을 복종치 않는 자들에게 형벌을 주시리니 이런 자들이 주의 얼굴과 그의 힘의 영광을 떠나 영원한 멸망의 형벌을 받으리로다 그 날에 강림하사 그의 성도들에게서 영광을 얻으시고 모든 믿는 자에게서 기이히 여김을 얻으시리라 (우리의 증거가 너희에게 믿어졌음이라)』

then you also will appear with him in glory.

1 Thessalonians 4:13-17 — Brothers, we do not want you to be ignorant about those who fall asleep, or to grieve like the rest of men, who have no hope. We believe that Jesus died and rose again and so we believe that God will bring with Jesus those who have fallen asleep in him. According to the Lord's own word, we tell you that we who are still alive, who are left till the coming of the Lord, will certainly not precede those who have fallen asleep. For the Lord himself will come down from heaven, with a loud command, with the voice of the archangel and with the trumpet call of God, and the dead in Christ will rise first. After that, we who are still alive and are left will be caught up together with them in the clouds to meet the Lord in the air. And so we will be with the Lord forever.

2 Thessalonians 1:7-10 — and give relief to you who are troubled, and to us as well. This will happen when the Lord Jesus is revealed from heaven in blazing fire with his powerful angels. He will punish those who do not know God and do not obey the gospel of our Lord Jesus. They will be punished with everlasting destruction and shut out from the presence of the Lord and from the majesty of his power on the day he comes to be glorified in his holy people and to be marveled at among all those who have believed. This

데살로니가후서 2:8 －『그 때에 불법한 자가 나타나리니 주 예수께서 그 입의 기운으로 저를 죽이시고 강림하여 나타나심으로 폐하시리라』

디모데전서 6:14 －『우리 주 예수 그리스도 나타나실 때까지 점도 없고 책망 받을 것도 없이 이 명령을 지키라』

히브리서 9:28 －『이와 같이 그리스도도 많은 사람의 죄를 담당하시려고 단번에 드리신 바 되셨고 구원에 이르게 하기 위하여 죄와 상관 없이 자기를 바라는 자들에게 두 번째 나타나시리라』

히브리서 10:37 －『잠시 잠깐 후면 오실 이가 오시리니 지체하지 아니하시리라』

- 요한을 통해

요한일서 2:28 －『자녀들아 이제 그 안에 거하라 이는 주께서 나타내신 바 되면 그의 강림하실 때에 우리로 담대함을 얻어 그 앞에서 부끄럽지 않게 하려 함이라』

요한일서 3:2 －『사랑하는 자들아 우리가 지금은 하나님의 자녀라 장래에 어떻게 될 것은 아직 나타나지 아니하였으나 그가 나타내심이 되면 우리가 그와 같을 줄을 아는 것은 그

includes you, because you believed our testimony to you.

2 Thessalonians 2:8 — And then the lawless one will be revealed, whom the Lord Jesus will overthrow with the breath of his mouth and destroy by the splendor of his coming.

1 Timothy 6:14 — to keep this command without spot or blame until the appearing of our Lord Jesus Christ,

Hebrews 9:28 — so Christ was sacrificed once to take away the sins of many people; and he will appear a second time, not to bear sin, but to bring salvation to those who are waiting for him.

Hebrews 10:37 — For in just a very little while, "He who is coming will come and will not delay.

— through John

1 John 2:28 — And now, dear children, continue in him, so that when he appears we may be confident and unashamed before him at his coming.

1 John 3:2 — Dear friends, now we are children of God, and what we will be has not yet been made known. But we know that when he appears, we shall be like him, for we

의 계신 그대로 볼 것을 인함이니』

요한계시록 1:7 -『볼지어다 구름을 타고 오시리라 각인의 눈이 그를 보겠고 그를 찌른 자들도 볼 터이요 땅에 있는 모든 족속이 그를 인하여 애곡하리니 그러하리라 아멘』

요한계시록 19:11-21 -『또 내가 하늘이 열린 것을 보니 보라 백마와 탄 자가 있으니 그 이름은 충신과 진실이라 그가 공의로 심판하며 싸우더라 그 눈이 불꽃 같고 그 머리에 많은 면류관이 있고 또 이름 쓴 것이 하나가 있으니 자기 밖에 아는 자가 없고 또 그가 피 뿌린 옷을 입었는데 그 이름은 하나님의 말씀이라 칭하더라 하늘에 있는 군대들이 희고 깨끗한 세마포를 입고 백마를 타고 그를 따르더라 그의 입에서 이한 검이 나오니 그것으로 만국을 치겠고 친히 저희를 철장으로 다스리며 또 친히 하나님 곧 전능하신 이의 맹렬한 진노의 포도주 틀을 밟겠고 그 옷과 그 다리에 이름 쓴 것이 있으니 만왕의 왕이요 만주의 주라 하였더라 또 내가 보니 한 천사가 해에 서서 공중에 나는 모든 새를 향하여 큰 음성으로 외쳐 가로되 와서 하나님의 큰 잔치에 모여 왕들의 고기와 장군들의 고기와 장사들의 고기와 말들과 그 탄 자들의 고기와 자유한 자들이나 종들이나 무론대소하고 모든 자의 고기를 먹으라 하더라 또 내가 보매 그 짐승과 땅의 임금들과 그 군대들이 모여 그 말 탄 자와 그의 군대로 더불어 전쟁을 일으키다가 짐승이 잡히고 그 앞에서 이적을 행하던 거짓 선지자도 함

shall see him as he is.

Revelation 1:7 — Look, he is coming with the clouds, and every eye will see him, even those who pierced him; and all the peoples of the earth will mourn because of him. So shall it be! Amen.

Revelation 19:11-21 — I saw heaven standing open and there before me was a white horse, whose rider is called Faithful and True. With justice he judges and makes war. His eyes are like blazing fire, and on his head are many crowns. He has a name written on him that no one knows but he himself. He is dressed in a robe dipped in blood, and his name is the Word of God. The armies of heaven were following him, riding on white horses and dressed in fine linen, white and clean. Out of his mouth comes a sharp sword with which to strike down the nations. "He will rule them with an iron scepter." He treads the winepress of the fury of the wrath of God Almighty. On his robe and on his thigh he has this name written : KING OF KINGS AND LORD OF LORDS. And I saw an angel standing in the sun, who cried in a loud voice to all the birds flying in midair, "Come, gather together for the great supper of God, so that you may eat the flesh of kings, generals, and mighty men, of horses and their riders, and the flesh of all people, free and slave, small and great." Then

께 잡혔으니 이는 짐승의 표를 받고 그의 우상에게 경배하던 자들을 이적으로 미혹하던 자라 이 둘이 산 채로 유황불 붙는 못에 던지우고 그 나머지는 말 탄 자의 입으로 나오는 검에 죽으매 모든 새가 그 고기로 배불리우더라』

요한계시록 22:20 -『이것들을 증거하신 이가 가라사대 내가 진실로 속히 오리라 하시거늘 아멘 주 예수여 오시옵소서』

I saw the beast and the kings of the earth and their armies gathered together to make war against the rider on the horse and his army. But the beast was captured, and with him the false prophet who had performed the miraculous signs on his behalf. With these signs he had deluded those who had received the mark of the beast and worshiped his image. The two of them were thrown alive into the fiery lake of burning sulfur. The rest of them were killed with the sword that came out of the mouth of the rider on the horse, and all the birds gorged themselves on their flesh.

Revelation 22:20 — He who testifies to these things says, "Yes, I am coming soon." Amen. Come, Lord Jesus.

장 12 재림 후 하늘에서 1000년간 성도들과 함께 심판하며 왕으로 계심

사 건	예언	
1. 요한을 통해 예언함	계시록 20:2, 4, 6, 12	
2. 바울을 통해 예언함	고린도전서 6:2	

– 요한을 통해

요한계시록 20:2, 4, 6, 12 -『[2] 용을 잡으니 곧 옛 뱀이요 마귀요 사단이라 잡아 일천 년 동안 결박하여 [4] 또 내가 보좌들을 보니 거기 앉은 자들이 있어 심판하는 권세를 받았더라 또 내가 보니 예수의 증거와 하나님의 말씀을 인하여 목베임을 받은 자의 영혼들과 또 짐승과 그의 우상에게 경배하지도 아니하고 이마와 손에 그의 표를 받지도 아니한 자들이 살아서 그리스도로 더불어 천 년 동안 왕 노릇 하니 [6] 이 첫째 부활에 참예하는 자들은 복이 있고 거룩하도다 둘째 사망이 그들을 다스리는 권세가 없고 도리어 그들이 하나님과 그리스도의 제사장이 되어 천 년 동안 그리스도로 더불어 왕 노릇 하리라 [12] 또 내가 보니 죽은 자들이 무론대소하고 그 보좌 앞에 섰는데 책들이 펴 있고 또 다른 책이 펴졌으니 곧 생명책이라 죽은 자들이 자기 행위를 따라 책들에

Chapter 12

Being a King and Judging with the Saints for 1000 Years in Heaven after the Second Coming

Event	Prophecy	
Prophesied through John	Revelation 20:2, 4, 6, 12	
Prophesied through Paul	1 Corinthians 6:2	

− **Prophesied through John**

Revelation 20:2, 4, 6, 12 — [2] He seized the dragon, that ancient serpent, who is the devil, or Satan, and bound him for a thousand years. [4] I saw thrones on which were seated those who had been given authority to judge. And I saw the souls of those who had been beheaded because of their testimony for Jesus and because of the word of God. They had not worshiped the beast or his image and had not received his mark on their foreheads or their hands. They came to life and reigned with Christ a thousand years. [6] Blessed and holy are those who have part in the first resurrection. The second death has no power over them, but they will be priests of God and of Christ and will reign with him for a thousand years. [12] And I saw the dead, great and small,

기록된 대로 심판을 받으니』

- 바울을 통해

　고린도전서 6:2 　-『성도가 세상을 판단할 것을 너희가 알지 못하느냐 세상도 너희에게 판단을 받겠거든 지극히 작은 일 판단하기를 감당치 못하겠느냐』

standing before the throne, and books were opened. Another book was opened, which is the book of life. The dead were judged according to what they had done as recorded in the books.

— Prophesied through Paul

> 1 Corinthians 6:2 — Do you not know that the saints will judge the world? And if you are to judge the world, are you not competent to judge trivial cases?

장 13 천년 후 지구로 돌아옴(세 번째 강림)

사 건	예언	역사적 연대
1. 새 예루살렘이 하늘에서 내려옴	스가랴 14:4; 요한계시록 21:2	
2. 사단이 옥에서 놓임 받음	요한계시록 20:3, 7	
3. 죽음 악인들이 부활함(둘째 부활)	욥기 21:30; 이사야 24:21-22 요한계시록 20:5, 13	
4. 부활한 악인들이 마귀와 그의 천사들을 위하여 예비된 불못에서 둘째 사망(영원히 소멸함)을 경험함	시편 11:6; 이사야 24:22, 34:2-4 욥기 21:30; 말라기 4:1, 3; 마태복음 25:41; 히브리서 12:29 베드로후서 3:10; 요한계시록 20:13-15, 21:8	
5. *사단, 타락한 천사들, 죄 그리고 사망이 영원히 소멸됨	이사야 25:8; 에스겔 28:18-19 요한계시록 20:14	

1. 새 예루살렘이 하늘에서 내려옴

스가랴 14:4 -『그 날에 그의 발이 예루살렘 앞 곧 동편 감람 산에 서실 것이요 감람 산은 그 한가운데가 동서로 갈라져 매우 큰 골짜기가 되어서 산 절반은 북으로, 절반은 남으로 옮기고』

요한계시록 21:2 -『또 내가 보매 거룩한 성 새 예루살렘이 하나님께로부터 하늘에서 내려오니 그 예비한 것이 신부가 남편을 위하여 단장한 것 같더라』

Chapter 13
Return to the Earth after the 1000 Years: the Third Coming

Event	Prophecy	Chronology
1. New Jerusalem Descends from Heaven	Zechariah 14:4; Revelation 21:2	
2. Satan Released from his Prison	Revelation 20:3, 7	
3. Wicked Dead Resurrected(Second Resurrection)	Job 21:30; Isaiah 24:21-22 Revelation 20:5, 13	
4. Resurrected Wicked Experience the Second Death(extinction forever) in the Lake of Fire Prepared for Satan and his Angels	Psalms 11:6; Isaiah 24:22, 34:2-4 Job 21:30; Malachi 4:1, 3 Matthew 25:41; Hebrews 12:29 2 Peter 3:10; Revelation 20:13-15, 21:8	
5. *Eternal Extinction of Satan, Fallen Angels, Sin, and Death	Isaiah 25:8; Ezekiel 28:18-19 Revelation 20:14	

1. New Jerusalem descends from Heaven

Zechariah 14:4 — On that day his feet will stand on the Mount of Olives, east of Jerusalem, and the Mount of Olives will be split in two from east to west, forming a great valley, with half of the mountain moving north and half moving south.

Revelation 21:2 — I saw the Holy City, the new Jerusalem, coming down out of heaven from God, prepared as a bride beautifully dressed for her husband.

2. 사단이 옥에서 놓임 받음

요한계시록 20:3, 7 — 『[3] 무저갱에 던져 잠그고 그 위에 인봉하여 천 년이 차도록 다시는 만국을 미혹하지 못하게 하였다가 그 후에는 반드시 잠간 놓이리라 [7] 천 년이 차매 사단이 그 옥에서 놓여』

3. 죽은 악인들이 부활함 (둘째 부활)

욥기 21:30 — 『악인은 남기워서 멸망의 날을 기다리움이 되고 멸망의 날을 맞으러 끌려 나감이 된다 하느니라』

이사야 24:21-22 — 『그 날에 여호와께서 높은 데서 높은 군대를 벌하시며 땅에서 땅의 왕들을 벌하시리니 그들이 죄수가 깊은 옥에 모임같이 모음을 입고 옥에 갇혔다가 여러 날 후에 형벌을 받을 것이라』

요한계시록 20:5, 13 — 『[5] (그 나머지 죽은 자들은 그 천 년이 차기까지 살지 못하더라) 이는 첫째 부활이라 [13] 바다가 그 가운데서 죽은 자들을 내어주고 또 사망과 음부도 그 가운데서 죽은 자들을 내어주매 각 사람이 자기의 행위대로 심판을 받고』

2. Satan released from his Prion

Revelation 20:3, 7 — [3] He threw him into the Abyss, and locked and sealed it over him, to keep him from deceiving the nations anymore until the thousand years were ended. After that, he must be set free for a short time. [7] When the thousand years are over, Satan will be released from his prison

3. Wicked Dead Resurrected (Second Resurrection)

Job 21:30 — that the evil man is spared from the day of calamity, that he is delivered from the day of wrath?

Isaiah 24:21–22 — In that day the LORD will punish the powers in the heavens above and the kings on the earth below. They will be herded together like prisoners bound in a dungeon; they will be shut up in prison and be punished after many days."

Revelation 20:5, 13 — "[5] (The rest of the dead did not come to life until the thousand years were ended.) This is the first resurrection. [13] The sea gave up the dead that were in it, and death and Hades gave up the dead that were in them, and each person was judged according to what he had done.

4. 부활한 악인들이 마귀와 그의 천사들을 위하여 예비된 불못에서 둘째 사망(영원히 소멸함)을 경험함

> 시편 11:6 — 『악인에게 그물을 내려 치시리니 불과 유황과 태우는 바람이 저희 잔의 소득이 되리로다』

> 이사야 24:22 — 『그들이 죄수가 깊은 옥에 모임 같이 모음을 입고 옥에 갇혔다가 여러 날 후에 형벌을 받을 것이라』

> 이사야 34:2-4 — 『대저 여호와께서 만국을 향하여 진노하시며 그들의 만군을 향하여 분내사 그들을 진멸하시며 살륙케 하셨은즉 그 살륙 당한 자는 내어던진바 되며 그 사체의 악취가 솟아오르고 그 피에 산들이 녹을 것이며 하늘의 만상이 사라지고 하늘들이 두루마리 같이 말리되 그 만상의 쇠잔함이 포도나무 잎이 마름 같고 무화과나무 잎이 마름 같으리라』

> 욥기 21:30 — 『악인은 남기워서 멸망의 날을 기다리움이 되고 멸망의 날을 맞으러 끌려 나감이 된다 하느니라』

> 말라기 4:1, 3 — 『[1] 만군의 여호와가 이르노라 보라 극렬한 풀무불 같은 날이 이르리니 교만한 자와 악을 행하는 자는 다 초개 같을 것이라 그 이르는 날이 그들을 살라 그 뿌리와 가지를 남기지 아니할 것이로되 [3] 또 너희가 악인을 밟을 것

4. **Resurrected Wicked Experience the Second Death (extinction forever) in the Lake of Fire Prepared for Satan and his Angels**

Psalms 11:6 — On the wicked he will rain fiery coals and burning sulfur; a scorching wind will be their lot.

Isaiah 24:22 — They will be herded together like prisoners bound in a dungeon; they will be shut up in prison and be punished after many days.

Isaiah 34:2-4 — The LORD is angry with all nations; his wrath is upon all their armies. He will totally destroy them, he will give them over to slaughter. Their slain will be thrown out, their dead bodies will send up a stench; the mountains will be soaked with their blood. All the stars of the heavens will be dissolved and the sky rolled up like a scroll; all the starry host will fall like withered leaves from the vine, like shriveled figs from the fig tree.

Job 21:30 — that the evil man is spared from the day of calamity, that he is delivered from the day of wrath?

Malachi 4:1, 3 — [1] 'Surely the day is coming; it will burn like a furnace. All the arrogant and every evildoer will be stubble, and that day that is coming will set them on fire,' says the LORD Almighty. 'Not a root or a branch will be left to

이니 그들이 나의 정한 날에 너희 발바닥 밑에 재와 같으리라 만군의 여호와의 말이니라』

마태복음 25:41 -『또 왼편에 있는 자들에게 이르시되 저주를 받은 자들아 나를 떠나 마귀와 그 사자들을 위하여 예비된 영영한 불에 들어가라』

히브리서 12:29 -『우리 하나님은 소멸하는 불이심이니라』

베드로후서 3:10 -『그러나 주의 날이 도적같이 오리니 그 날에는 하늘이 큰 소리로 떠나가고 체질이 뜨거운 불에 풀어지고 땅과 그 중에 있는 모든 일이 드러나리로다』

요한계시록 20:13-15 -『바다가 그 가운데서 죽은 자들을 내주고 또 사망과 음부도 그 가운데서 죽은 자들을 내어주매 각 사람이 자기의 행위대로 심판을 받고 사망과 음부도 불못에 던지우니 이것은 둘째 사망 곧 불못이라 누구든지 생명책에 기록되지 못한 자는 불못에 던지우더라』

요한계시록 21:8 -『그러나 두려워하는 자들과 믿지 아니하는 자들과 흉악한 자들과 살인자들과 행음자들과 술객들과 우

them. [3] Then you will trample down the wicked; they will be ashes under the soles of your feet on the day when I do these things,' says the LORD Almighty.

Matthew 25:41 — "Then he will say to those on his left, 'Depart from me, you who are cursed, into the eternal fire prepared for the devil and his angels.

Hebrews 12:29 — for our "God is a consuming fire."

2 Peter 3:10 — But the day of the Lord will come like a thief. The heavens will disappear with a roar; the elements will be destroyed by fire, and the earth and everything in it will be laid bare.

Revelation 20:13-15 — The sea gave up the dead that were in it, and death and Hades gave up the dead that were in them, and each person was judged according to what he had done. Then death and Hades were thrown into the lake of fire. The lake of fire is the second death. If anyone's name was not found written in the book of life, he was thrown into the lake of fire.

Revelation 21:8 — But the cowardly, the unbelieving, the vile, the murderers, the sexually immoral, those who practice

상 숭배자들과 모든 거짓말하는 자들은 불과 유황으로 타는 못에 참예하리니 이것이 둘째 사망이라』

5. 사단, 타락한 천사들, 죄, 사망 그리고 지구도 영원히 소멸됨*

이사야 25:8 −『사망을 영원히 멸하실 것이라 주 여호와께서 모든 얼굴에서 눈물을 씻기시며 그 백성의 수치를 온 천하에서 제하시리라 여호와께서 이같이 말씀하셨느니라』

에스겔 28:18-19 −『네가 죄악이 많고 무역이 불의하므로 네 모든 성소를 더럽혔음이여 내가 네 가운데서 불을 내어 너를 사르게 하고 너를 목도하는 모든 자 앞에서 너로 땅 위에 재가 되게 하였도다 만민 중에 너를 아는 자가 너로 인하여 다 놀랄 것임이여 네가 경계거리가 되고 네가 영원히 다시 있지 못하리로다 하셨다 하라』

요한계시록 20:14 −『사망과 음부도 불못에 던지우니 이것은 둘째 사망 곧 불못이라』

---

*창세기 3:15 - "그(예수)는 너(사탄)의 머리를 상하게 할 것이요…"에 예언한 대로 예수는 최후로 그의 약속을 성취하셨다. 예수는 우리를 죄의 형벌과 권능에서뿐만 아니라 죄의 존재로부터 구원하는 메시아(그리스도)다.

magic arts, the idolaters and all liars-their place will be in the fiery lake of burning sulfur. This is the second death."

5. Eternal Extinction of Satan, Fallen Angels, Sin, and Death*

Isaiah 25:8 — he will swallow up death forever. The Sovereign LORD will wipe away the tears from all faces; he will remove the disgrace of his people from all the earth. The LORD has spoken.

Ezekiel 28:18-19 — By your many sins and dishonest trade you have desecrated your sanctuaries. So I made a fire come out from you, and it consumed you, and I reduced you to ashes on the ground in the sight of all who were watching. All the nations who knew you are appalled at you; you have come to a horrible end and will be no more.

Revelation 20:14 — Then death and Hades were thrown into the lake of fire. The lake of fire is the second death.

---

*As prophesied in Genesis 3:15 -"…he [Jesus] will crush your [Satan's] head…." Jesus finally fulfills His promise. Jesus is the Messiah (Christ) who saves believers not only from the penalty and power of sin but also ultimately from its very existence.

장 14 새 하늘과 새 땅을 창조하심

사 건	예언	역사적 연대
1. 다윗을 통해 예언함	시편 37:11	
2. 이사야를 통해 예언함	이사야 11:6-9, 32:18, 35:1-2, 65:17, 22-23	
3. 베드로를 통해 예언함	베드로후서 3:13	
4. 요한을 통해 예언함	*요한계시록 21:1, 5-6	

1. 다윗을 통해 예언함

시편 37:11 -『오직 온유한 자는 땅을 차지하며 풍부한 화평으로 즐기리로다』

2. 이사야를 통해 예언함

이사야 11:6-9 -『그 때에 이리가 어린 양과 함께 거하며 표범이 어린 염소와 함께 누우며 송아지와 어린 사자와 살찐 짐승이 함께 있어 어린 아이에게 끌리며 암소와 곰이 함께 먹으며 그것들의 새끼가 함께 엎드리며 사자가 소처럼 풀을 먹을 것이며 젖먹는 아이가 독사의 구멍에서 장난하며 젖뗀 어린 아이가 독사의 굴에 손을 넣을 것이라 나의 거룩한 산 모든 곳에서 해됨도 없고 상함도 없을 것이니 이는 물이 바다를 덮음

Chapter

14 Creation of New Heaven and Earth

Event	Prophecy	Chronology
1. Prophesied through David	Psalms 37:11	
2. Prophesied through Isaiah	Isaiah 11:6-9, 32:18, 35:1-2, 65:17, 22-23	
3. Prophesied through Peter	2 Peter 3:13	
4. Prophesied through John	*Revelation 21:1, 5-6	

1. Prophesied through David

Psalms 37:11 — But the meek will inherit the land and enjoy great peace.

2. Prophesied through Isaiah

Isaiah 11:6-9 — The wolf will live with the lamb, the leopard will lie down with the goat, the calf and the lion and the yearling together; and a little child will lead them. The cow will feed with the bear, their young will lie down together, and the lion will eat straw like the ox. The infant will play near the hole of the cobra, and the young child put his hand into the viper's nest. They will neither harm nor destroy

같이 여호와를 아는 지식이 세상에 충만할 것임이니라』

이사야 32:18 -『내 백성이 화평한 집과 안전한 거처와 종용히 쉬는 곳에 있으려니와』

이사야 35:1-2 -『광야와 메마른 땅이 기뻐하며 사막이 백합화같이 피어 즐거워하며 무성하게 피어 기쁜 노래로 즐거워하며 레바논의 영광과 갈멜과 사론의 아름다움을 얻을 것이라 그것들이 여호와의 영광 곧 우리 하나님의 아름다움을 보리로다』

이사야 65:17, 22-23 -『[17] 보라 내가 새 하늘과 새 땅을 창조하나니 이전 것은 기억되거나 마음에 생각나지 아니할 것이라 [22-23] 그들의 건축한 데 타인이 거하지 아니할 것이며 그들의 재배한 것을 타인이 먹지 아니하리니 이는 내 백성의 수한이 나무의 수한과 같겠고 나의 택한 자가 그 손으로 일한 것을 길이 누릴 것임이며 그들의 수고가 헛되지 않겠고 그들의 생산한 것이 재난에 걸리지 아니하리니 그들은 여호와의 복된 자의 자손이요 그 소생도 그들과 함께 될 것임이라』

3. 베드로를 통해 예언함

베드로후서 3:13 -『우리는 그의 약속대로 의의 거하는 바 새

on all my holy mountain, for the earth will be full of the knowledge of the LORD as the waters cover the sea.

Isaiah 32:18 — My people will live in peaceful dwelling places, in secure homes, in undisturbed places of rest.

Isaiah 35:1-2 — The desert and the parched land will be glad; the wilderness will rejoice and blossom. Like the crocus, it will burst into bloom; it will rejoice greatly and shout for joy. The glory of Lebanon will be given to it, the splendor of Carmel and Sharon; they will see the glory of the LORD, the splendor of our God.

Isaiah 65:17, 22-23 — "[17] "Behold, I will create new heavens and a new earth. The former things will not be remembered, nor will they come to mind. [22-23] No longer will they build houses and others live in them, or plant and others eat. For as the days of a tree, so will be the days of my people; my chosen ones will long enjoy the works of their hands. They will not toil in vain or bear children doomed to misfortune; for they will be a people blessed by the LORD, they and their descendants with them."

3. Prophesied through Peter

2 Peter 3:13 — "But in keeping with his promise we are

하늘과 새 땅을 바라보도다』

4. 요한을 통해 예언함

*요한계시록 21:1, 5-6 —『[1] 또 내가 새 하늘과 새 땅을 보니 처음 하늘과 처음 땅이 없어졌고 바다도 다시 있지 않더라 [5-6] 보좌에 앉으신 이가 가라사대 보라 내가 만물을 새롭게 하노라 하시고 또 가라사대 이 말은 신실하고 참되니 기록하라 하시고 또 내게 말씀하시되 이루었도다 나는 알파와 오메가요 처음과 나중이라 내가 생명수 샘물로 목마른 자에게 값없이 주리니』

---

*이사야 9:7 – "그 정사와 평강의 더함이 무궁하며 또 다윗의 위에 앉아서 그 나라를 굳게 세우고 자금 이후 영원토록 공평과 정의로 그것을 보존하실 것이라 만군의 여호와의 열심이 이를 이루시리라"에서 예언한 대로 주님은 그의 약속을 최후로 성취한다.

looking forward to a new heaven and a new earth, the home of righteousness."

4. Prophesied through John

*Revelation 21:1, 5-6 — "[1] Then I saw a new heaven and a new earth, for the first heaven and the first earth had passed away, and there was no longer any sea. [5-6] He who was seated on the throne said, "I am making everything new!" Then he said, "Write this down, for these words are trustworthy and true." He said to me : "It is done. I am the Alpha and the Omega, the Beginning and the End. To him who is thirsty I will give to drink without cost from the spring of the water of life."

---

*As prophesied in Isaiah 9:7 — "Of the increase of His government and peace There will be no end, Upon the throne of David and over His kingdom, To order it and establish it with judgment and justice From that time forward, even forever. The zeal of the Lord of hosts will perform this.." The Lord finally fulfills His promise.

최고의 기쁜 소식

우리의 조상 아담이 선악을 알게 하는 나무의 실과를 먹음으로써(창세기 3:6), 최대의 기만자, 사단을 순종하였을 때 죄가 이 세상에 들어오게 되었다. "이러므로 한 사람으로 말미암아 죄가 세상에 들어오고 죄로 말미암아 사망이 왔나니 이와 같이 모든 사람이 죄를 지었으므로 사망이 모든 사람에게 이르렀느니라"(로마서 5:12). 그렇지만, "한 범죄로 많은 사람이 정죄에 이른 것같이 의의 한 행동으로 말미암아 많은 사람이 의롭다 하심을 받아 생명에 이르렀느니라 한 사람의 순종치 아니함으로 많은 사람이 죄인 된 것같이 한 사람의 순종하심으로 많은 사람이 의인이 되리라"(로마서 5:18-19).

여기서 말하는 의의 한 사람은 예수 그리스도 즉 출생 전에 자서전을 쓴 자다. 예수는 창조주로서 "태초에 하나님과 함께 계셨고" 또한 "만물이 그로 말미암아 지은 바 되었다"(요한복음 1:2-3). 예수는 사람이 되어 이 땅에서 살았던 하나님이다(요한복음 1:14).

그는 이 땅에 살았을 때 한 번도 범죄한 일이 없었으며 성경에 기록된 대로 하나님의 뜻을 온전히 순종하였다(요한일서 3:5; 히브리서 10:7). 죄가 없으신 예수는 우리로 하여금 저의 안에서 하나님의 의가 되게 하려고 우리를 대신하여 죄가 되셨다(고린도후서 5:21). 십자가에서 예수 그리스도는 자신을 온 세상을 위한 화목제물로 바침으로 우리가 거룩함을 입게 되었고(히브리서 10:10) "한 제물로 거룩하게

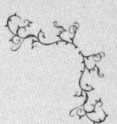

The Best Good News

Sin entered this world when our ancestor Adam obeyed the greatest deceiver, Satan, and destroyed his relationship with God by eating the fruit of the tree of knowledge of good and evil (Gen. 3:6). "Therefore, ··· sin entered the world through one man, and death through sin, and in this way death came to all men, because all sinned" (Rom. 5:12). Nevertheless, "just as the result of one trespass was condemnation for all men, so also the result of one of righteousness was justification that brings life for all men" (Rom. 5:18-19).

This "one of righteousness" is Jesus Christ, the man who wrote his autobiography before he was born. Jesus is the creator "who was with God in the beginning," and "through him all things were made" (John 1:2-3). Jesus, who is God, became a human and lived on earth (John 1:14).

He is called the righteous one because while on earth he never sinned, and he fully obeyed the will of God as stated in the Bible (Heb. 10:7; 1 John 3:5). Jesus, the sinless one, was made "to be sin for us, so that in him we might become the righteousness of God" (2 Cor. 5:21). On the cross, Jesus Christ offered himself as the sacrifice

된 자들을 영원히 온전케 하셨"(히브리서 10:14)다. 복된 소식은 우리가 그분을 전심으로 믿고 순종할 때 예수께서 하나님 아버지를 순종함으로 받은 보상과 영광이 우리의 것이 될 수 있다는 것이다(히브리서 5:9; 요한계시록 3:21). 그러므로 인류를 위한 궁극적인 희망은 예수 그리스도를 개인의 구원자며 주님으로 믿을 뿐만 아니라 그분을 전심으로 신뢰하며 순종하는 삶을 사는 것이다.

예수는 성경이 자기에 관하여 증거한다고 말하였다(요한복음 5:39). 이와 같은 주장은 우리에게 예수가 성경 전체의 중심임을 이해하도록 한다. 성경은 창세기부터 요한계시록에 이르기까지 그의 역사(History)이다. 예수가 출생 전에 그의 자서전을 쓴 목적은, 즉 사람들로 하여금 예수는 "그리스도시요 살아 계신 하나님의 아들"임을 믿게 하며 멸망치 않고 영생을 얻게 함이다(마태복음 16:16; 요한복음 3:16, 20:31).

for the world, by which we have been made holy (Heb. 10:10), and "he has made perfect forever those who are being made holy" (Heb. 10:14). The good news is that Jesus' reward and glory which he received after his ascension will be ours when we believe and obey him (Heb. 5:9; Rev. 3:21). Therefore, the ultimate hope for humankind is to understand who Jesus Christ is, and to have a personal relationship with him as their Savior and Lord, and to trust and obey him wholeheartedly.

Jesus claimed that the Scriptures testified of him (John 5:39), which identifies him as the center of the Bible. The Bible is his story, revealed from Genesis to Revelation. Jesus' purpose in writing his autobiography before he was born is for people to believe in him as "the Christ, the son of the living God" and have eternal life (Matthew 16:16; John 3:16, 20:31).

호 소

우리는 전쟁, 자연재해, 경제위기, 기근, 질병, 범죄, 사망이 가득한 세상에서 살고 있다. 죄가 세상에 들어온 이후로 인류는 오랫동안 이와 같은 문제들을 해결하고자 노력하고 있다. 그렇지만 지구에서 일어나는 모든 문제의 유일한 해결책은 예수께서 다시 오시는 것인데 그때에는 악인들이 멸망하고 죽은 의인들이 죽지 않을 몸으로 부활하며 산 신자들이 불멸의 몸으로 변화되어 승천할 것이다(고린도전서 15:51-54; 데살로니가전서 4:14-17 참조). 그러므로 예수 그리스도가 이 지구상에 모든 사람에게 가능한 가장 빨리 소개되어지는 것이 최고로 중요한 것임에 틀림 없다.

예수의 사역에 관한 지금까지의 모든 예언들은 다 성취되었다. 그러므로 마지막 일곱 재앙부터 새 하늘과 새 땅이 창조되는 미래에 대한 예언들이 모두 다 성취될 것은 명약관화한 일이다. 그리고 우리는 성경에 기록된 주님의 말씀을 순종함으로써 속히 오실 예수의 재림을 준비하도록 서로 노력해야 할 것이다.

"사랑하는 자들아 주께는 하루가 천년 같고 천 년이 하루 같은 이 한 가지를 잊지 말라 주의 약속은 어떤 이의 더디다고 생각하는 것같이 더딘 것이 아니라 오직 너희를 대하여 오래 참으사 아무도 멸망치 않고 다 회개하기에 이르기를 원하시느니라 그러나 주의 날이 도적같이 오리니 그 날에는 하늘이 큰

 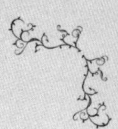

APPEAL

We are living in a world filled with wars, natural disasters, economic crises, diseases, starvation, and death. Humans have been trying to solve these problems for a long time, ever since sin entered the earth. However, the only lasting solution for all the problems happening on earth is Jesus' second coming. Upon Jesus' return, the wicked will perish, the righteous dead will be raised imperishable, and the living believers will be changed into immortality (1 Cor. 15:52, 54; 1Thes. 4:14-17). Therefore, it is extremely important that Jesus and his second coming be introduced to all people on earth as soon as possible.

All prophecies up till now in regard to Jesus' ministries have been fulfilled. Therefore, we can be confident that all the remaining prophecies about the second coming and the new heaven and earth will come to pass. Let us help each other to be ready for his soon coming by following the word of our Lord in the scriptures.

> But do not forget this one thing, dear friends: With the Lord a day is like a thousand years, and a thousand years are like a day. The Lord is not slow in keeping his promise, as some understand slowness. He is patient with you,

소리로 떠나가고 체질이 뜨거운 불에 풀어지고 땅과 그 중에 있는 모든 일이 드러나리로다 이 모든 것이 이렇게 풀어지리니 너희가 어떠한 사람이 되어야 마땅하뇨 거룩한 행실과 경건함으로 하나님의 날이 임하기를 바라보고 간절히 사모하라 그 날에 하늘이 불에 타서 풀어지고 체질이 뜨거운 불에 녹아지려니와 우리는 그의 약속대로 의의 거하는 바 새 하늘과 새 땅을 바라보도다"
(베드로후서 3:8-13).

우리가 위에서 성경 구절을 읽은 바대로 사도 베드로는
(1) " 거룩한 행실과 경건함으로…"
(2) 하나님의 날이 임하기를 바라보고 오심을 촉진시키라"(speed its coming, NIV)고 권면하였다.

그렇다면 우리는 어떻게 거룩한 행실과 경건함으로 살 수 있을까? 여기에 그 비결이 있다: "일을 아니할지라도 경건하지 아니한 자를 의롭다 하시는 이를 믿는 자에게는 그의 믿음을 의로 여기시나니"(로마서 4:5)라는 진리를 믿음으로써 그리고 하나님의 계명과 예수 믿음을 지킴으로써(요한계시록 14:12) 우리의 구세주와의 관계를 지속할 수 있다. 우리는 어떻게 그분의 오심을 촉진시킬 수 있는가? 예수께서 승천하시기 전에 제자들에게, "그리스도 중심의 제자 훈련"(Christ Centered Discipleship)이 담긴 대 사명 (마태복음 28:18-20)을 위임하셨다.

우리는 어떻게 예수께서 분부하신 대 사명을 순종할 수 있을까? 우리는 곱하기 법의 원칙을 적용하여 모든 나라와 족속과 방언과 백성에게 때를 따라 영적인 양식을 나누어주며 성령의 능력을 통하여 그리스도의 충성되고 참된 증인의 사역을 충실히 수행함으로

not wanting anyone to perish, but everyone to come to repentance. But the day of the Lord will come like a thief. The heavens will disappear with a roar; the elements will be destroyed by fire, and the earth and everything in it will be laid bare. Since everything will be destroyed in this way, what kind of people ought you to be? You ought to live holy and godly lives as you look forward to the day of God and speed its coming. That day will bring about the destruction of the heavens by fire, and the elements will melt in the heat. But in keeping with his promise we are looking forward to a new heaven and a new earth, the home of righteousness.

2 Peter 3:8-13(NIV)

As we saw in the scripture quoted above, the Apostle Peter states that:

(1) "You ought to live holy and godly lives," and

(2) "look forward to the day of God, and speed its coming."

How can we lead holy and godly lives? Here is the secret: We can maintain our relationship with our Savior by believing the truth that "To him who does not work but believes on Him who justifies the ungodly, his faith is accounted for righteousness"(Romans 4:5) and keeping "the commandments of God and the faith of Jesus"(Rev. 14:12). How can we speed up His coming? Before Jesus ascended to heaven, he gave his disciples the great commission (Matt. 28:18-20) which involves Christ-centered discipleship.

How can we fulfill Jesus' great commission? We can work towards accomplishing his great commission by sharing the spiritu-

대 사명을 완수할 수 있다(사도행전 1:8; 요한계시록 3:14, 14:6; 마태복음 24:14, 45).

곱하기 법의 기본적 원칙은 다음의 예화가 잘 설명한다.

한 아버지는 두 아들에게 오는 일 년 동안 어떻게 임금을 지불할 지에 관하여 물어 보았다. 그는 저들에게 두 가지 선택 즉 (1) 매주일 천 불씩 혹은 (2) 첫 주에는 1불을 주되 매주마다 그 전 주일의 배를 셈하여 주는 것 두 가지를 제안하였다. 장남은 매주 천 불씩 받는 것을 택했고 차남은 지혜롭게도 곱하기의 두 번째 원칙을 선택하였다. 이 이야기를 실제로 적용한다면 그해 끝에 장남은 5만 2천 달러를 받는 반면 차남은 22조 5179억 9678만 7632달러를 받게 될 것이다. 얼마나 엄청난 차이인가. 이 차이는 더하기 법과 대조적인 곱하기 법칙의 능력을 보여주는 것이다.

이 대 사명(마태복음 28:18-20)의 실질적 적용은 다음과 같다. 즉, 한 사람이 출생 전에 자서전을 쓴 사람에 관한 이 팸플릿을 두 사람에게 나누어 주며 또한 저들이 그리스도 중심의 제자가 되도록 조력하는 것이다. 그리고 그 두 사람은 그것을 각각 다른 두 사람에게 나누어주고 또 저들이 그리스도 중심의 제자가 되도록 도와 주는 것이다. 이 과정이 바로 더하기 법이 아닌 곱하기 법의 원칙에 기초한 것이다.

우리가 교파와 국경을 초월하여 이렇게만 계속 한다면 조만간 수백만, 수천만의 사람들이 출생 전에 자서전을 쓴 사람을 알게 되며 그분에 의해 변화될 것이다. 이 팸플릿을 받는 모든 사람들은 영원 구원 사업에 곱하기 법의 원칙을 사용하여 그리스도의 재림을 촉진

al food at the proper time with every nation, tribe, language, and people, using the principle of multiplication, and becoming Christ's faithful and true witnesses through the power of the Holy Spirit (Acts 1:8; Rev. 3:14, 14:6; Matt. 24:14, 45).

The following is an illustration of the basic principle of multiplication. A father asked his two sons how they wanted him to pay them for the coming one year's work. He gave them two choices: (1) $1,000 per week or (2) $1 for the first week after which the amount would be doubled every week. The first son chose to take the $1,000 per week, and the second son who was wise to the principle of multiplication decided to take the second option. At the end of the year, the first son received $52,000 while the second son received $22,517,996,787,632. What a contrast! The difference shows the power of multiplication as contrasted with addition.

A practical application of this multiplication principle to the great commission(Matt. 28:18-20) is for everyone to share this message and booklet with at least two people, thereby making them Christcentered disciples. They in turn are also to share it with at least two other people, and help them to become Christ-centered disciples. This process is based on the principle of multiplication, not addition. If we actively continue to engage in fulfilling Jesus' great commission beyond any denominational and national boundaries, then very soon, thousands and even millions of people will learn of and be transformed by the Man who wrote his

시키는 것이 바로 나의 기도이다.

"이 예언의 말씀을 읽는 자와 듣는 자와 그 가운데에 기록한 것을 지키는 자는 복이 있나니 때가 가까움이라"(요한계시록 1:3).

autobiography before he was born. It is my prayer that everyone who receives this booklet will engage in the principle of multiplication for bringing people to Jesus and will work towards hastening Jesus' second coming.

> "Blessed is the one who reads the words of this prophecy, and blessed are those who hear it and take to heart what is written in it, because the time is near." (Revelation 1:3)

출생 전에 자서전을 쓴 사람
The man who wrote his autobiography before he was born

1판 1쇄 인쇄 _ 2017년 9월 25일
1판 1쇄 발행 _ 2017년 9월 30일

지은이 _ 조명수
펴낸이 _ 이형규
펴낸곳 _ 쿰란출판사

주소 _ 서울특별시 종로구 이화장길 6
편집부 _ 745-1007, 745-1301~2, 747-1212, 743-1300
영업부 _ 747-1004, FAX 745-8490
본사평생전화번호 _ 0502-756-1004
홈페이지 _ http://www.qumran.co.kr
E-mail _ qrbooks@gmail.com / qrbooks@daum.net
한글인터넷주소 _ 쿰란, 쿰란출판사
등록 _ 제1-670호(1988.2.27)
책임교열 _ 김유미

ⓒ 조명수 2017   ISBN 978-89-6562-996-2 93230

책값은 뒤표지에 있습니다.
이 출판물은 저작권법에 의해 보호를 받는 저작물이므로 무단 복제할 수 없습니다.
파본(破本)은 구입처에서 교환해 드립니다.

The price of this book is on the back cover page. No part of this publication may be reproduced without permission as it is protected by copyright. The damaged book may be exchanged at the place of purchase.